ABOUT THE BOOK

This book was designed for the students who are aspiring for MBA/CAT/XAT/CMAT/MAT/SNAP/KMAT/IIFT/GATE/ICET Examination. For cracking these exams, basics are very important. So before stepping into your real tests, you should have complete knowledge regarding all the topics that you are being tested for the examination

AF487529

Intended Audience

This book is ideal for MBA/CAT/XAT/CMAT/MAT/SNAP/KMAT/IIFT/GATE/ICET students. All the topics contained in this book are available as the Animated Videos in www.testprep24.com. So the book along with the videos will make your preparation easier.

How to read this book

As we have animated videos for this book at www.testprep24.com , you will get good result if you read this book simultaneously by watching videos.

Structure of each topic

All the topics in this book are discussed from the root. Initially we teach all the basics associated with the particular topic then followed by relevant examples along with explanatory answers. So it will be easy for the students to solve the questions what they come across in the competitive exams.

Index

1. Numbers

3. Geometry **Page 77- Page 109**

5. Counting **Page 128- Page 159**

6. Statistics **Page 160- Page 180**

NUMBERS

Numbers

1) Numbers Classification

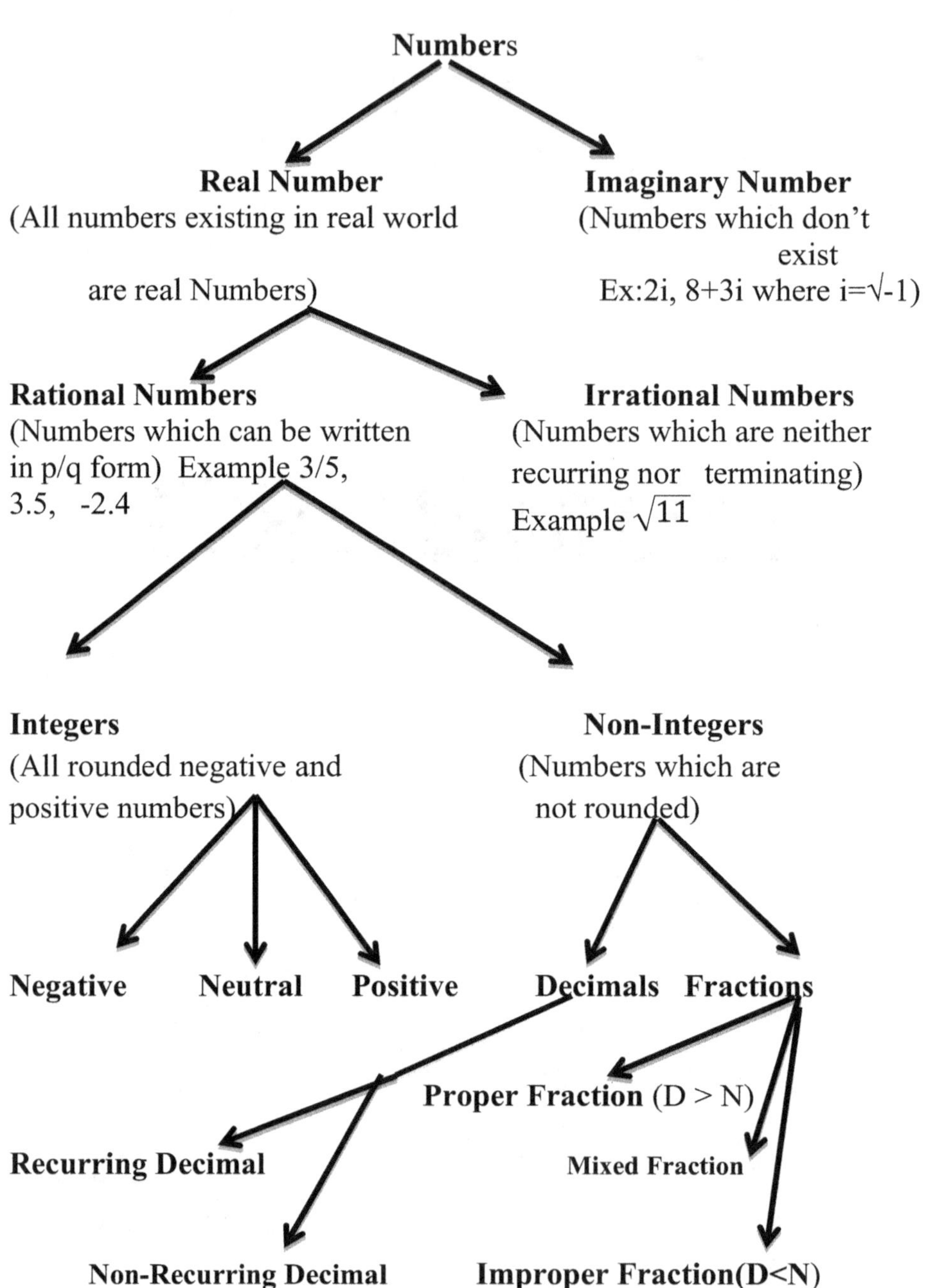

2) <u>Integers Classification</u>

Integers

Even

(Integer divided by '2' gives 0 as a remainder)
Example {4, 10, 44,}

Odd

(Integer divided by '2' gives 1 as a remainder)
Example {1, 3, 5, 9}

Positive Integers

Natural Number
{1, 2, 3.......}

Whole Number
{0, 1, 2............}

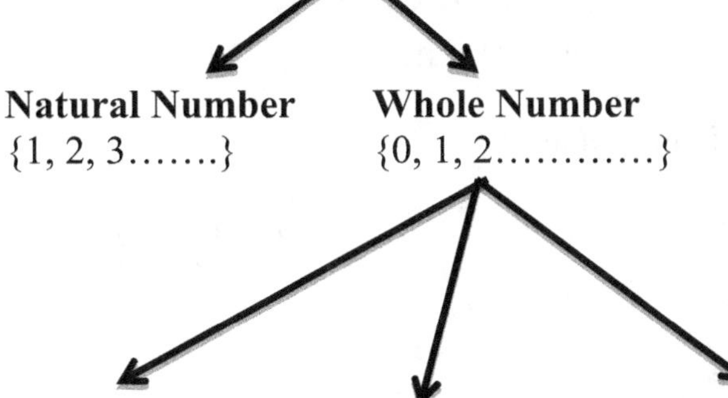

Neither Prime nor Composite
(Numbers with less than more 2 factors)
Ex {0, 1}

Prime Number
(Numbers with exactly 2 factors one and itself)
Ex {2, 3, 5}

Composite Number
(Numbers with than 2 factors)
Ex {4, 6, 8}

Even Prime
(Combination of even and and prime
Ex: {2}

Co-Prime
(Two number with'1' as a common factor)
Ex: {(14, 15), (2, 3), (5, 7)}

Twin-Prime
(difference b/w two prime number is 2)
Ex: (5, 7)

3) Perfect Number and Fibonacci sequence

a) Perfect Number

If sum of all factors of a number (excluding the number) is equal to the number then it is a perfect number.

Example:-

6 has the factors 1, 2 ,3 and 6.

When we add 1,2,3 excluding 6, the sum will be equal to 6.

1+2+3=6, so 6 is a perfect number.

b) Fibonacci sequence

The sequence where you get your next number by adding two previous numbers.

Example:-
0, 1, 1, 2, 3, 5, 8…………………………..

4) BODMAS

B O D M A S

Bracket of Division Multiplication Addition Subtraction

The order has to be followed while solving a question.

Example:-

Solve $45 \div (5 \times 3) - 6 \times 2 + 5 - (3 - 2)$
$45 \div 15 - 6 \times 2 + 5 - 1$
$3 - 6 \times 2 + 5 - 1$
$3 - 12 + 5 - 1$
$3 - 7 - 1$
-5

5) Decimals and Fractions

a) Place Values of Decimals

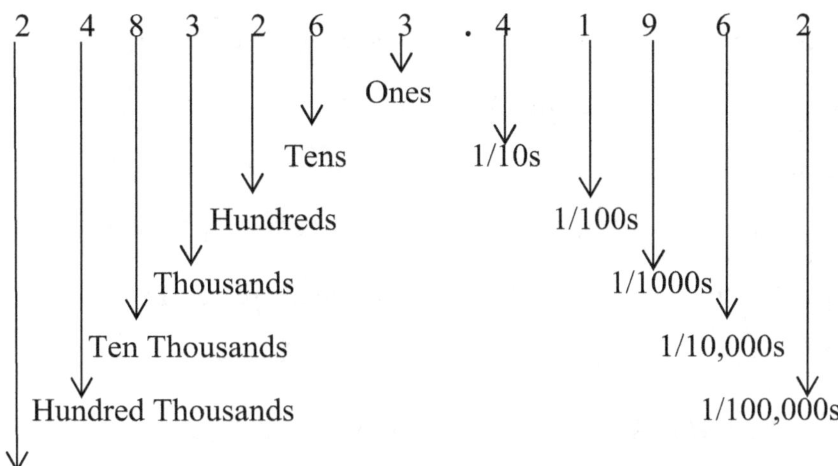

Millions

Millions = 10^6

Billions = 10^9

Trillions = 10^{12}

Example:-

Find the place and face value of 9 in 248.41962

Sol:-

Place value of '9'= 9/1000= 0.009 (Value of the number as per its place)

Face value of '9'= 9 (Without considering the place whatever the value is called as face value)

Example:-

If x= 248.4196, find the value of x rounded to the nearest hundreds, tens, units, tenths, hundredths, thousandths.

Hundreds	=200 (In 248.4196 here '4' is less than '5')
Tens	=250 (In 248.4196 here '8' is greater than '5')
Units	=248 (After decimal point value is less than'5')
Tenths	=248.4 (After '4' value is less than '5')
Hundredths	= 248.42 (After '1' value is greater than '5')
Thousandths	= 248.420 (After '9' value is greater than '5')

b) Converting Decimals to Fractions and vice versa:

Example:-

Convert 326.87 to fraction

$$326.87 \times \frac{100}{100} = \frac{32687}{100}$$

Example:-

Convert $3.\bar{6}8$ to Fraction

$Here\ x = 3.6868\bar{6}8$

$$\begin{aligned} 100x &= 368.6868\bar{6}8 \\ \_\_\ x &= 3.6868\bar{6}8 \\ \hline 99x &= 365.0 \end{aligned}$$

$$x = \frac{365}{99}$$

c) Addition and Subtraction of Fractions:-

$$\frac{3}{5}-\frac{7}{15}+\frac{9}{10}$$

Here try to make denominators equal. Good number for 5, 10, 15 is 30 (L.C.M of numbers)

$$=\frac{3}{5}\times\frac{6}{6}-\frac{7}{15}\times\frac{2}{2}+\frac{9}{10}\times\frac{3}{3}$$

$$=\frac{18}{30}-\frac{14}{30}+\frac{27}{30}$$

$$=\frac{18-14+27}{30} = \frac{31}{30}$$

d) Multiplication and Division of Fractions

$$\frac{3}{5}\times\frac{7}{15}=\frac{7}{25}$$

$$\frac{\frac{3}{5}}{\frac{7}{15}}=\frac{3}{5}\times\frac{15}{7}=\frac{9}{7}$$

$$\frac{\frac{3}{5}}{\frac{7}{1}}=\frac{3}{5}\times\frac{1}{7}=\frac{3}{35}$$

e) Conversion of Proper Fraction to Mixed Fraction and Vice versa

Proper Fraction to Mixed Fraction

$$\frac{10}{7}$$

$$7)\ 10\ (1$$
$$\underline{7}$$
$$3$$

$$= 1\frac{3}{7}$$

$$1\frac{3}{7} = \frac{7 \times 1 + 3}{7} = \frac{10}{7}$$

f) Addition and Subtraction of Mixed Fractions

Example:-

$$= 999\frac{4}{7} + 999\frac{3}{5} + 999 + 999\frac{2}{5} + 999\frac{3}{7}$$

Add the integer separately and fraction separately

$$= 999 + 999 + 999 + 999 + 999 + (\frac{4}{7} + \frac{3}{5} + \frac{2}{5} + \frac{3}{7})$$

$$= 4995 + 2 = 4997$$

6) Factors and Multiples

Multiples:-

The numbers which we get after multiplying the number by integer values.

Factors:-

The numbers what all we can multiply to get the number.

Example:-

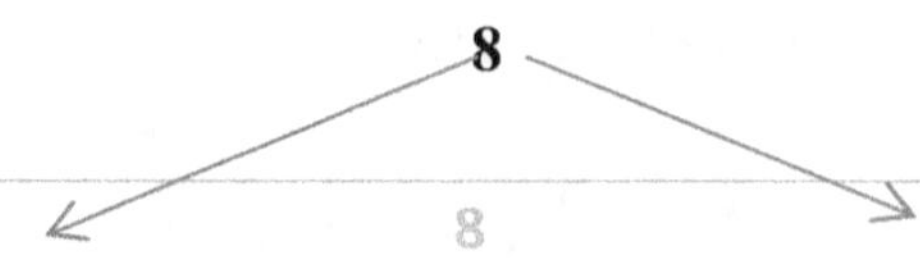

1, 2, 4, 8	8, 16, 24, 32………..
(In what all tables you get '8' as a number are called as factors)	(In 8 table what all numbers you get are called as multiples)

7) L.C.M and H.C.F

a) Method-1

L.C.M (Least Common Multiple) H.C.F (Highest Common Factor)

L.C.M (4, 6, 8)	H.C.F (4, 6, 8)
4 = 4, 8, 12, 16, 20, **24,**…44,**48**…	4 = **1**, **2**, 4
6 = 6, 12, 18, **24** ,30,36,42,**48**…...	6 = **1**, **2**, 3, 6
8 = 8, 16, **24**, 32, 40,**48**………	8 = **1**, **2**, 4, 8
Step1: Write the multiples	Step1: Write the Factors
Step2: Pick the common and least number	Step2: Pick the common and highest number
Here L.C.M = 24	Here H.C.F = 2

b) Method 2

Find the L.C.M and H.C.F of 32, 54, and 96

32 = 2 x 16

2 x 8

2 x 4

2 x 2

$32 = 2 \times 2 \times 2 \times 2 \times 2 = 2^5$

54= 2 x 27

3 x 9

3 x 3

$54 = 2 \times 3 \times 3 \times 3 = 2 \times 3^3$

96= 2 x 48

2 x 24

2 x 12

2 x 6

2 x 3

$96 = 2 \times 2 \times 2 \times 2 \times 2 \times 3 = 2^5 \times 3^1$

L.C.M: Multiply all the highest power values

H.C.F: Multiply all the least power values

$$32 = 2^5 \times 3^0$$
$$54 = 2^1 \times 3^3$$
$$96 = 2^5 \times 3^1$$

$$L.C.M = 2^5 \times 3^3 = 864$$
$$H.C.F = 2^1 \times 3^0 = 2$$

c) Method-3

Find the L.C.M and H.C.F of 32, 54 and 96.

L.C.M:-

2	32, 54, 96
3	16, 27, 48
16	16, 9, 16
9	1, 9, 1
	1, 1, 1

$2 \times 3 \times 16 \times 9 \times 1 \times 1 \times 1 = 864$

H.C.F:-

Initially pick any two numbers and find the H.C.F then find the H.C.F of result with third number.

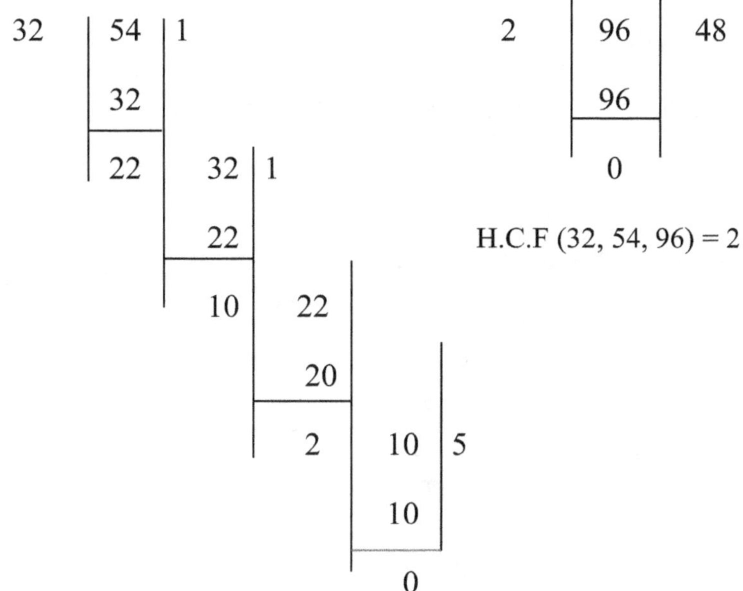

H.C.F = (32, 54) = 2

d) Points to be noted on L.C.M and H.C.F

$(i) L.C.M\,(a,b) \times H.C.F(a,b) = a \times b$

(ii) $L.C.M\left(\frac{x}{a}, \frac{y}{b}, \frac{z}{c}\right) = \frac{L.C.M(x,y,z)}{H.C.F(a,b,c)}$

$(iii) H.C.F\left(\frac{x}{a}, \frac{y}{b}, \frac{z}{c}\right) = \frac{H.C.F(x,y,z)}{L.C.M(a,b,c)}$

$(iv) a^x \times b^y \times c^z$ (If a, b, c are prime factors).

$$number\ of\ factors = (x+1)(y+1)(z+1)$$

$$Sum\ of\ factors = \frac{a^{x+1}-1}{a-1} \times \frac{b^{y+1}-1}{b-1} \times \frac{c^{z+1}-1}{c-1}$$

Example:-

Find the sum of factors and number of factors for 480?

480 = 2 x 240

2 x 120

2 x 60

2 x 30

2 x 15

3 x 5

$480 = 2 \times 2 \times 2 \times 2 \times 2 \times 3 \times 5 = 2^5 \times 3^1 \times 5^1$

Here

Number of factors = (5+1) (1+1) (1+1)

= 6 x 2 x 2

= 24 factors

$$Sum\ of\ factors = \frac{2^{5+1}-1}{(2-1)} \times \frac{3^{1+1}-1}{(3-1)} \times \frac{5^{1+1}-1}{(5-1)}$$

$$Sum\ of\ factors = \frac{2^{6}-1}{1} \times \frac{3^{2}-1}{2} \times \frac{5^{2}-1}{4}$$

$$Sum\ of\ factors = \frac{64-1}{1} \times \frac{9-1}{2} \times \frac{25-1}{4}$$

$$Sum\ of\ factors = \frac{63}{1} \times \frac{8}{2} \times \frac{24}{4}$$

$$Sum\ of\ factors = 1512$$

7) Factorials:

1. Find the number of zeros in 20! (Or) find the maximum power 10 in 20! ?

Solution:

20! = 20 x 19 x 18 x 17.................................x 3 x 2 x 1

In order to get zero we need '5' and '2'.

So identify all the numbers where you get '5' or '0'. A combination of '5' and '2' will give you a Zero.

(Here no need to check for '2' because in all even numbers you get '2', so count for total number of 5's)

5, 10, 15, 20 these are the places where you can get '5'. '5' multiplied with '2' will give you a 'zero'.

So the number of Zeros is '4'.

2. Find the number of zeros in 100!

Solution:

Let's write down the place where you get '5'

5	10	15	20	25
30	35	40	45	50
55	60	65	70	75
80	85	90	95	100

Here in the above 20 numbers we get '5'

25 = 5 x 5 50 = 5 x 5 x 2

75 = 5 x 5 x 3 100 = 5 x 5 x 4

There are 4 places where you get an extra '5'

So total number of fives = 20+4 =24

So the total number of zeros = 24

3. Find the maximum power of '6' in 100!
Solution:

To get '6' we need '2' and '3'.

To find number of prime numbers in a factorial value we will go for continuous division of number. And sum of all the values give the result.

2	100
2	50
2	25
2	12
2	6
2	3
	1
Total	97

3	100
3	33
3	11
3	3
	1
Total	48

$$100! = 2^{97} \times 3^{48} \times M$$
$$= 6^{48} \times 2^{49} \times M$$

(Here we get 48 sixes in 100!)

9) Divisibility Rules

2 → Last number should be divisible by '2'

$4(2^2)$ → Last two numbers should be divisible by '4'

$8(2^3)$ → Last three numbers should be divisible by '8'

3 → Sum of the digits in the number should be divisible by '3'

9(3^2) → Sum of the digits in the number should be divisible by '9'

5 → Last digit in a number should be '0' or '5'

10 → Last digit in a number should be '0'

6 → Number should be divisible by '2' and '3'

12 → Number should be divisible by '3' and '4'

11 → The difference between the sum of the alternative digits from left to right should be '0' or divisible by '11'

7 → Double the last digit and subtract from the remaining number continuously if the number left is divisible by '7' then entire number is divisible by '7'.

Example:

Check 34685 is divisible by which all numbers

Solution:

Two: 5/2 (not divisible by '2' because last digit is not divisible by '2')

Three: 3+4+6+8+5 = 26/3 (not divisible by '3' because Sum of the digits in the number are not divisible by '3')

Four: 85/4 (not divisible by '4'because last two numbers are not

divisible by '4')

Five: '5' (last digit is '5' so number is divisible by '5')

Six: 2, 3 does not satisfy so not divisible by '6'

Seven:

```
3 4 6 8 | 5
        | X
    -10 | 2
-----------
        | 10
  3 4 5 | 8
        | X
   -1 6 | 2
-----------
        | 16
    3 2 | 9
        | X
    -18 | 2
-----------
     14 | 18
```

$\frac{14}{7}$ (Left out digit is divisible by '7' so number is divisible by '7')

Eight: 685/8 (Not divisible by '8' because last three numbers are not divisible by '8')

Nine: 3+4+6+8+5 = 26/9 (not divisible by '9' because the sum of digits is not divisible by '9')

Ten: last digit is '5' (not divisible by '10')

Eleven: (3+6+5) – (4+8) = 14-12 = 2 (Not divisible by '11')

Twelve: Not divisible by '3' (so the number is not divisible by '12')

ARITHMETIC

Percentages

a) What is Percentage

Per / Cent

(Anything we calculate with respect to 100 is called a percentage.)

Example:

A student scored 400 marks out of 500 marks. What is the percentage of marks obtained by the student?

Solution:

$$\frac{400}{500} = \frac{???}{100} =$$

$$(the\ score\ for\ 100\ marks\ is\ called\ as\ percentage)$$

$$\frac{400}{500} = \frac{80}{100} (If\ the\ same\ exam\ was\ written\ for\ 100\ marks\ his\ score\ will\ be\ 80\ marks\ So\ it\ is\ 80\%)$$

b) Why we need Percentage

For the purpose of comparison we use percentages.

Example:

A boy scored 400 marks out of 500 marks and girl scored 600 marks out of 1000. Who scored better?

Boy

$$\frac{400}{500} \times 100 = 80\%$$

Girl

$$\frac{600}{1000} \times 100 = 60\%$$

(So boy scored better. For the comparison purpose we use percentages.)

c) Finding Percentage

$$Percentage = \frac{obtain}{total} \times 100$$

Example:

A student scored 70 marks out of 80 marks in English, 50 out of 60 in science, 100 out of 100 in math and 35 out of 60 in social. Find the percentage of marks scored by student?

Solution:

$$Percentage = \frac{obtain}{total} \times 100$$

$$Percentage = \frac{70 + 50 + 100 + 35}{300} \times 100$$

$$Percentage = \frac{255}{300} \times 100$$

$$Percentage = 85\%$$

d) Percentage Change

$$Percentage\ change = \frac{change}{original} \times 100$$

Example:

A student scored 350 marks this year and his target score for next year is 450 marks, what percentage of marks should the student improve?

Solution:

$$\% \, change = \frac{450 - 350}{350} \times 100$$

$$\% \, change = \frac{100}{350} \times 100$$

$$\% \, change = \frac{200}{7} \%$$

e) Percentage to Fraction conversions:

Percentage Fraction

30% -------------/100--------------→ $\frac{30}{100}$

Fraction Percentage

$\frac{30}{100}$ --------------x100---------------→30%

f) Example Problems

1. $20\%\ of\ 600 = ?$

Solution:

$$100\% = 600$$

10%=60

$$20\% = 120$$

2. $39\%\ of\ 700 = ?$

Solution: $100\% = 700$

10% = 70

$$40\% - 1\% = 280 - 7 = 273$$

3. $250\%\ of\ 300 = ?$

Solution:

$$100\% = 300$$

$$100\% = 300$$

$$50\% = 150$$

$$250\% = 750$$

4. $20\ \%\ \ of\ 40\ \%\ \ of\ 350 = ?$

Solution: Start solving from right to left

$$40\ \%\ \ of\ 350$$

$$100\% = 350$$

10% = 35

$$\times 4 = \quad \times 4$$

$$40\% = 140$$

$20\%\ of\ 140$

$$100\% = 140$$

$$10\% = \ 14$$

So $20\% = 28$

5. $10\%\ \ of\ 20\%\ \ of\ 30\%\ \ of\ 40\%\ \ of\ 50\%\ \ of\ 4000 = ?$

Solution:

$50\%\ of\ 4000$

$$= \frac{50}{100} \times 4000$$

$$= 2000$$

$40\%\ 0f\ 2000$

$$= \frac{40}{100} \times 2000$$

$$= 800$$

$30\%\ of\ 800$

$$= \frac{30}{100} \times 800$$

$$= 240$$

$20\%\ of\ 240$

$$= \frac{20}{100} \times 240$$

$$= 48$$

$10\% \; of \; 48$

$$= \frac{10}{100} \times 48$$

$$= 4.8$$

So $10\% \;\; of \; 20\% \;\; of \; 30\% \;\; of \; 40\% \;\; of \; 50\% \;\; of \; 4000 = 4.8$

Example:

If price of a shirt reduced by 30%, 20% then find the resultant price of shirt?

Solution:

M.R.P = 3000$

100% = 3000$

30% ↓ -900

100% = 2100$

20% ↓ -420

Final value = 1680$

Example:

If the price of television is $8000 and increased by 30% and reduced by 50% and increased by 10%. Find the final price?

Solution:

M.R.P = 8000$

100 % = 8000

↑ 30% ↓ +2400

100%= 10,400

↓ 50% ↓ -5,200

100%= 5200

↑ 10% ↓ +520

5720/-

Example:

If price of a product is decreased by 20% then increased by 50%, 30% and reduced by 10% find the overall change in the product?

Solution: M.R.P = x

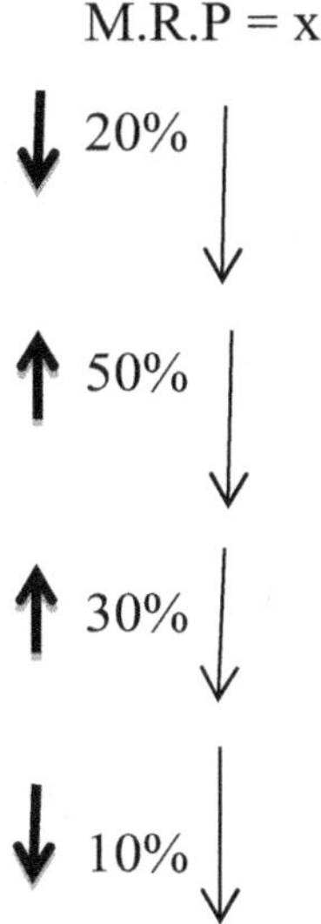

In this question there is no initial value, let's start with $100x$

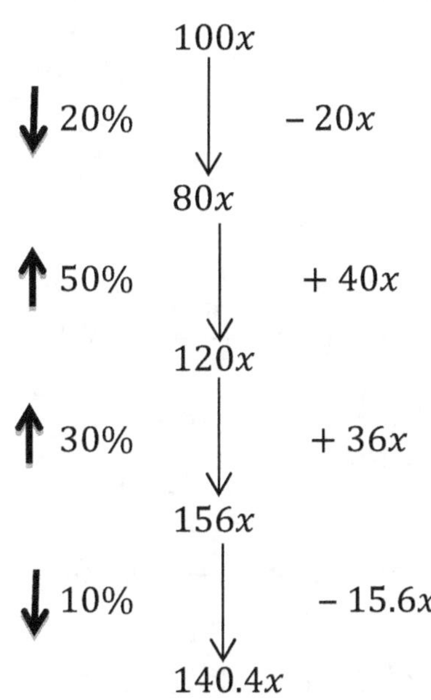

$$\% \, change = \frac{change}{initial} \times 100$$

$$\% \, change = \frac{140.4x - 100x}{100x} \times 100$$

$$\% \, change = \frac{40.4x}{100x} \times 100$$

$\% \, change = 40.4\%$ (Increase)

Example:

If price of a mobile is increased by 25%, in order to bring back the mobile's cost to its original value what percentage should it be reduced?

Solution:
Let us take the original price of mobile is $100x$

$100x$

+25% ↓ =+25x

$125x$

↓

$100x$

$$\% \, change = \frac{change}{initial} \times 100$$

$$\% \, change = \frac{125x - 100x}{125x} \times 100$$

$$\% \, change = \frac{25x}{125x} \times 100$$

$\% \, change = 20\% \, decrease$

To bring back to its previous price it has to be reduced by 20%.

Example:

If population of a city is increased by 10% and 20% then it is reduced by 50%, if the final population in the city is 2,64,000 then find the original population of the city?

Solution:

Let $100x$ be original position

$$100x$$

+10% ↓ =+10x

$$110x$$

+ 20% ↓ + 22x

$$132x$$

- 50% ↓ - 66x

$$66x$$

66x = 2,64,000

X = 2,64,000/66 = 4000

So

100(4000) = 400,000/- Original Population

Profit and Loss

a) The topics what we come across in Profit and Loss are

- Cost Price
- Selling Price
- Marked Price
- Profit
- Loss
- Discount
- Profit %
- Loss %
- Discount %

b) Relation between the above said terms:

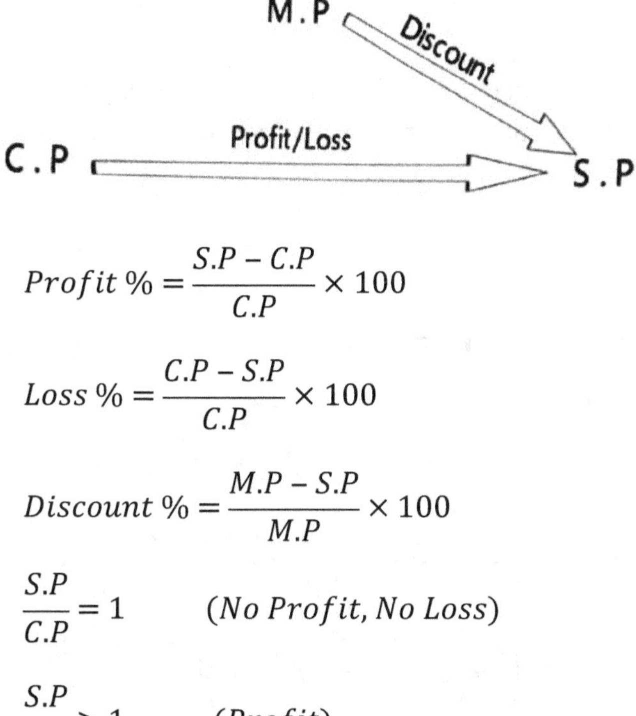

$$Profit\ \% = \frac{S.P - C.P}{C.P} \times 100$$

$$Loss\ \% = \frac{C.P - S.P}{C.P} \times 100$$

$$Discount\ \% = \frac{M.P - S.P}{M.P} \times 100$$

$$\frac{S.P}{C.P} = 1 \qquad (No\ Profit, No\ Loss)$$

$$\frac{S.P}{C.P} > 1 \qquad (Profit)$$

$$\frac{S.P}{C.P} < 1 \qquad (Loss)$$

c) Example Problems

Example: If S.P = 500 &C.P = 400 then find profit/loss percentage?

$$\frac{500}{400} = 1.25 \qquad (25\ \%\ profit)$$

Example: If S.P = 400 &C.P = 500 then find profit/loss percentage?

$$\frac{400}{500} = 0.80 \qquad (20\ \%\ Loss)$$

Example:

After allowing a discount of 20% the person is expecting a profit of 20%. If marked price of the product is $600 then find the cost price of the product?

Solution:

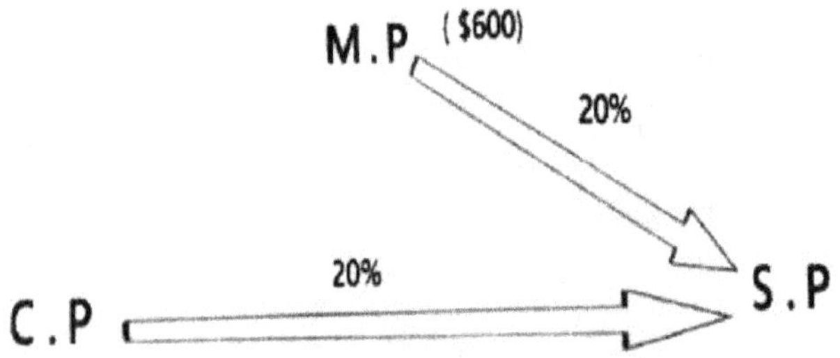

M.P ($600)
20%
20%
C.P
S.P

$$c.p\left(\frac{100+20}{100}\right) = s.p = 600\left(\frac{100-20}{100}\right)$$

$$c.p \times \frac{120}{100} = 600 \times \frac{80}{100}$$

$c.p = 400\$$

Example:

If the cost price of 10 pens is equal to the selling price of 8 pens then find the profit or loss percentage in the transaction?

Solution:

$$c.p\ (10\ pens\ ) = s.p\ (8\ pen)$$

$$\frac{s.p}{c.p} = \frac{10}{8} = 1.25$$

(25 % Profit)

Example:

A person bought two mobiles for the same price. on the first mobile he obtained a profit of 30% and on the second mobile he obtained a loss of 20% then find the overall profit or loss percentage in this transaction?

Solution:

C.P (M1) = 100 C.P (M2) = 100 T.C.P = 200

30% ↓ +30 20% ↓ -20

S.P (M1) = 130 S.P (M2) = 80 T.S.P = 210

$$P\% = \frac{S.P - C.P}{C.P} \times 100$$

$$P\% = \frac{210 - 200}{200} \times 100$$

$$P\% = \frac{10}{200} \times 100$$

$$P\% = 5\%$$

Example:

A person sold two mobiles for the same price, on the first mobile he obtained a profit of 30% and on the second mobile he obtained a loss of 20% then find overall profit or loss percentage in this transaction?

Solution:

Let C.P (M1) = 100x   C.P (M2) = 100y

C.P (M1) = 100x   C.P (M2) = 100y

↓ +30%   ↓ -20%

130x   80y

(As both the Selling prices are equal let us take the Selling price value as which is convenient to 130 and 80)

130x S.P (M1) = 13 x 8   80y S.P (M2) = 13x 8   T.S.P = 208

100x =80   100y =130

T.C.P=210

$$\% \, change = \frac{change}{initial} \times 100 =$$

$$\frac{210 - 208}{210} \times 100 = \frac{20}{21}\% \text{ loss}$$

Example:

After the successive discounts of 30% and 40% a person bought a car for $126,000. Then find the initial price of the car before discount?

Solution: Here we don't know the Initial Price so let us take it as 100x

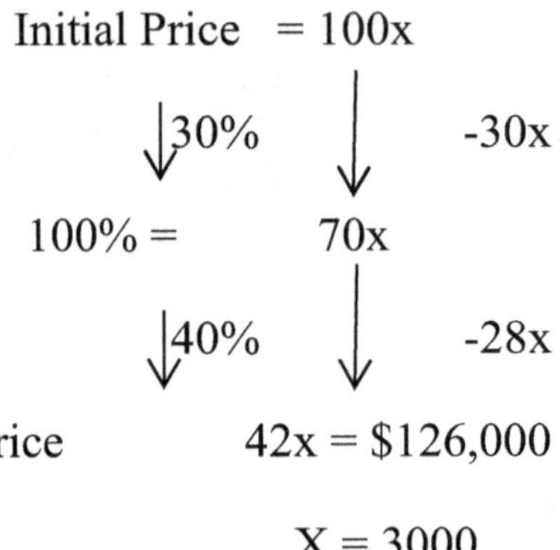

Given final price 42x = $126,000

X = 3000

So initial price is 100x = 100 x 3000 = 3,00,000/-

Simple Interest and Compound Interest

a) Simple Interest:-

If interest is calculated on the initial value every year it is called simple interest.

b) Compound Interest:-

If interest is calculated on amount (value plus interest) it is called as compound interest.

c) Basic Formulas

If a person give a Principal (P) for a time period (T) at a rate of interest per annum (R) then the final value returned by other person is called as Amount.

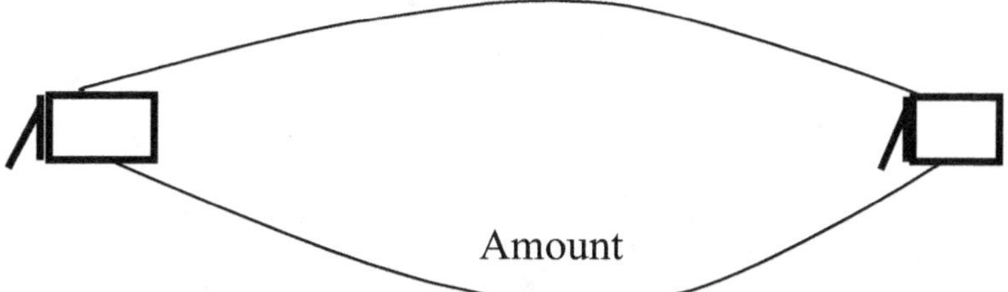

If it is given for simple interest $Amount = P + S.I$

If it is given for Compound interest $Amount = P + C.I$

$$Simple\ Interest = \frac{PTR}{100}$$

$$\text{Amount} = \text{P} + \frac{PTR}{100}$$

$$\text{Amount in Compound Interest} = P\left(1 + \frac{R}{100}\right)^T$$

Compound Interest= Amount - Principal

Amount in Compound Interest $= P\left(1 + \frac{R}{n * 100}\right)^{n * T}$

Where n = no of times we will compound in 1 year

If compound for every four months then n=3 (1 Year = 3* 4 months)

d) Examples:

If a person give a principal of 5000$, for a certain period at a rate of 20% per annum the values changes as shown below.

Let Principal=5000 Rate of Interest=20% Time = 3 years

S.I	C.I (for every 1 year)	C.I(for every 6 months)
100% = 5000	100% = 5000	100% = 5000
20% +1000	20% +1000	
6000	100% = 6000	6 month =10% +500
20% +1000	20% +1200	100% = 5500 (After 6 months)
7000	100% = 7200	
20% +1000	20% +1440	10% +550
8000	8640	100% = 6050(After 1year)
		10% +605
		1.5 years= 6655 (After 1.5 year)
(In simple Interest Interest for each year Is constant)	(In Compound Interest Interest is calculated on interest also)	(Here interest on interest is calculated for every 6 months)

Ratio and Proportion

a) What is the difference between ratio and a fraction

Ratio is a part to part relationship.

Boys: Girls = 3: 4

Fraction is a part to whole relationship.

$$Boy's\ fraction = \frac{3}{7}$$

$$Girl's\ fraction = \frac{4}{7}$$

b) Why Ratio

Giving relation between values in simplest possible way.

Example:

In Class A =500 students ,Class B = 700 students.

The simplest possible relation between A and B is 5:7

c) Division of Value as per Ratio

A: B: C = 3: 4: 5 Total = $36,000

Total Parts = 3+4+5=12 parts =$36,000

1 part =$3,000

So A's value = 3 x 3000 = 9,000

So B's value = 4 x 3000 = 12,000

So C's value = 5 x 3000 = 15,000

d) Combining Ratios

Example 1: In a Class1 Boys to Girls ratio is 4:3 and Class 2 Boys to Girls ratio is 1:2. Then find the Ratio of Boys to Girls in Class1 and 2 together?

Class 1 → Boys: Girls = 4: 3
Class 2 → Boys: Girls = 1: 2

Class 1 & 2 → Boys: Girls = 5: 5 = 1:1 Here we can't add ratios directly because

C1	→ B: G	=4B, 3G	(or)	8B, 6G
C2	→B: G	=1B, 2G	(or)	4B, 8G
		5: 5		12: 14

So for different values different ratios are possible. So Boys to Girls ratio can't be find.

Example2: If

$x{:}y = 1{:}2$
$y{:}z = 3{:}4$
$z{:}w = 5{:}1$ then find the value of x:y:z?

Here $x{:}y = 1{:}2$
$y{:}z = 3{:}4$ (Both y values are not equal let's equate both y values)

$3{:}6 \leftarrow x{:}y = (1{:}2)3$
$6{:}8 \leftarrow y{:}z = (3{:}4)2$ (To make them equal multiply with 2, 3)

$3{:}6{:}8 \leftarrow x{:}y{:}z$

$x{:}y{:}z = 3{:}6{:}8$ (Both z values are not equal let's equate both z values)

$z{:}w = 5{:}1$

$15{:}30{:}40 \leftarrow x{:}y{:}z = (3{:}6{:}8)5$ (To make both z values as equal
$40{:}8 \leftarrow z{:}w = (5{:}1)8$ multiply with 5, 8)

$15{:}30{:}40{:}8 = x{:}y{:}z{:}w$

e) **Proportion:**

For \$50 you get 10 chocolates then for \$70 you get 14 chocolates

So $50\${:}\ 10\ chocolates \quad :: \quad 70\${:}\ 14\ chocolates$

We will say all the values are in Proportion

$50{:}10 :: 70{:}14$

When values are in proportion product of mean is equal to product of extremes.

$50 \times 14 = 10 \times 70$

(i)Mean proportion $a{:}x{::}x{:}b$

$x^2 = ab,\ \ x = \sqrt{ab}$

Here x in mean proportion

(ii)Third proportion $a{:}b{::}b{:}x$

Here x in third proportion

(iii)Fourth proportion $a{:}b{::}c{:}x$

Here x in fourth proportion

f) <u>Direct Proportion and Indirect Proportion:</u>

(i)Direct Proportion:

When speed of a car increases distance travelled by the car also increases, so they are in direct proportion

$$Speed \propto Distance$$

Speed = k. distance (when we remove proportion we add a constant)

(ii) Inverse Proportion:-

When heat increases water level decreases. It is inverse proportion.

$$Heat \propto \frac{1}{Water\ level}$$

$$Heat\ = k.\frac{1}{water\ level}$$

$$(when\ we\ remove\ proportion\ we\ add\ a\ constant)$$

AVERAGES

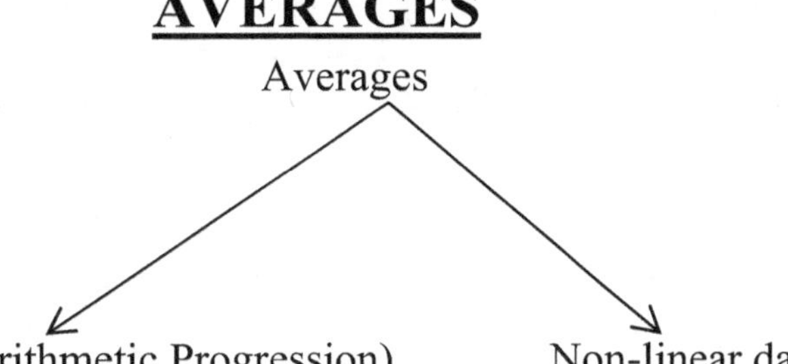

(a) Linear Data

If the given data is in Arithmetic Progression going with a constant
difference then

$$Average = \frac{first\ number + last\ number}{2}$$

Average = Middle Number (if there are odd number of numbers)

$Average = \ Average\ of\ middle\ numbers$ (If there are even number of numbers)

1. What is the average of numbers 1, 2, 3, 4, 5

$$Avg = \frac{first\ number + last\ number}{2} = \frac{1+5}{2}$$

$$Avg = \frac{6}{2}$$ or

$$Avg = \ Middle\ number = 3$$

Example:-

Find the average of first 200 positive even numbers.

Solution:-

Positive even numbers start from '2'

2, 4, 6, 8 ……………………..

So first number is 2(1) = 2

So last number is 2(200) = 400

$$Average = \frac{first\ number + last\ number}{2}$$

$$Average = \frac{2 + 400}{2} = 201$$

Example 2:-

The average of 10 consecutive odd numbers is '92'. Then find the second highest number in the sequence.

Solution:-

Given numbers are in sequence. And contains even number of digits so

$Average = Avg\ of\ middle\ numbers$

It means the average of two consecutive Odd numbers are 92, so the numbers are 91 and 93.

Then the sequence appears as follows

83, 85, 87, 89, 91, 93, 95, 97, **99**, 101

92

So 99 is the second highest number in the sequence.

(b)Non Linear data:

Here values are not in order, in such cases

$$Avg = \frac{Sum\ of\ observations}{Nuumber\ of\ observations}$$

(c)Weighted Average:

$$Average = \frac{m \times A + n \times B + \dots}{m + n \dots\dots\dots\dots}$$

m, n → no of items

A, B → value of the items

Example:-

In a class there are 250 Boys, 120 Girls and 30 Teachers. If average weight of Boys is 12kgs, Girls is 8kgs and Teachers is 60kgs. Then find the average weight of class.

Solution:

$$Average = \frac{m \times A + n \times B + \dots}{m + n \dots\dots\dots\dots}$$

$$Average = \frac{250 \times 12 + 120 \times 8 + 30 \times 60}{250 + 120 + 30}$$

$$Average = \frac{3000 + 960 + 1800}{400}$$

$$Average = \frac{5760}{400} = 14.4kgs$$

Example:

The average score of 11 players in Indian cricket team is 40 runs, the average score of first 6 players is 50 runs and average score of last 6 players is 35 runs. Then find the score of the 6th player?

Solution:-

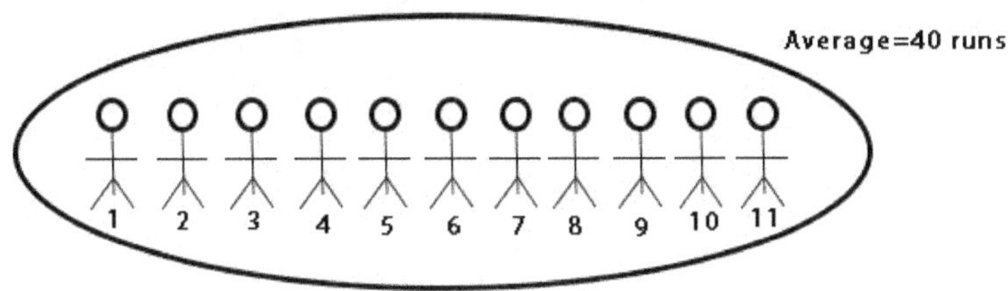

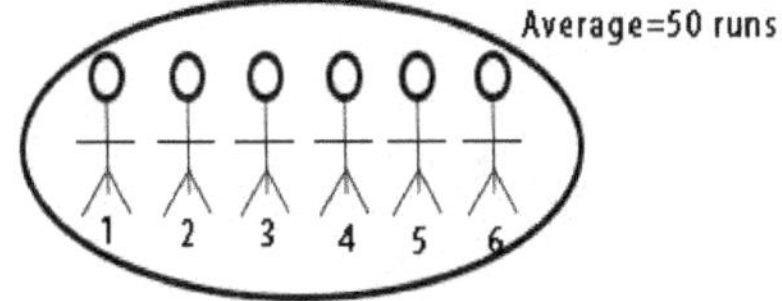

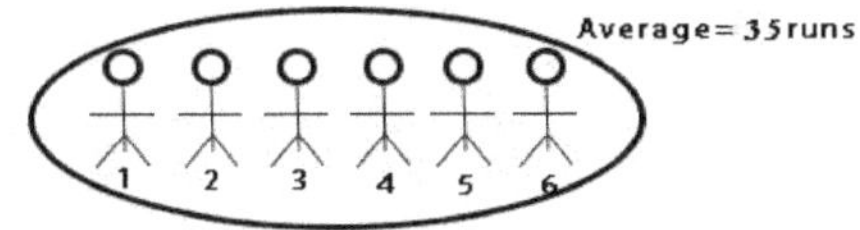

So in 2nd case 6th player score is appearing twice so.

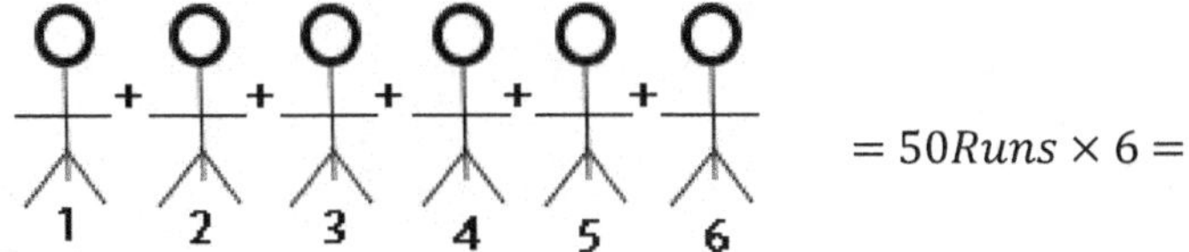

$= 50Runs \times 6 = 300Runs$

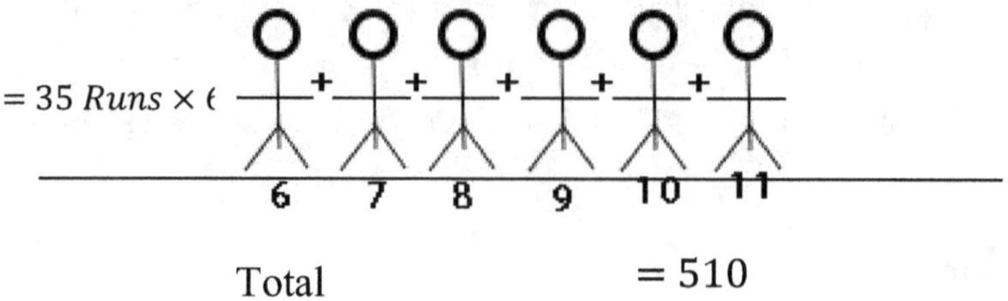

Total $= 510$

1 + 2 + 3 + 4 + 5 + 6 + 7 + 8 + 9 + 10 + 11 $= 40 Runs \times 11 = 440$

6th Player score $= 510 - 460 = 50 Runs$

Example:

The average weight of a class of 20 students is 30 kgs, due to entry of a new student the average weight increased by 1 kg, find the weight of the new student?

Solution:-

Total weight of 20 students = 20 x 30 = 600 kgs

Total weight of 21 students = 21 x 31 = 651 kgs

Difference = 651 – 600 = 51

Weight of a new student is 51 kgs

Mixtures and Allegations:

Mixtures

a) What is a mixture

When two or more substances are poured in a single vessel, we call the resultant as a mixture.

Examples:

1. Two equal vessels contain milk to water ratio as 2:3 and 3: 4, if both the vessels are mixed, what is the ratio of milk and water in the resulting vessel?

Solution:

Quantity in vessel 1 Quantity in vessel 2

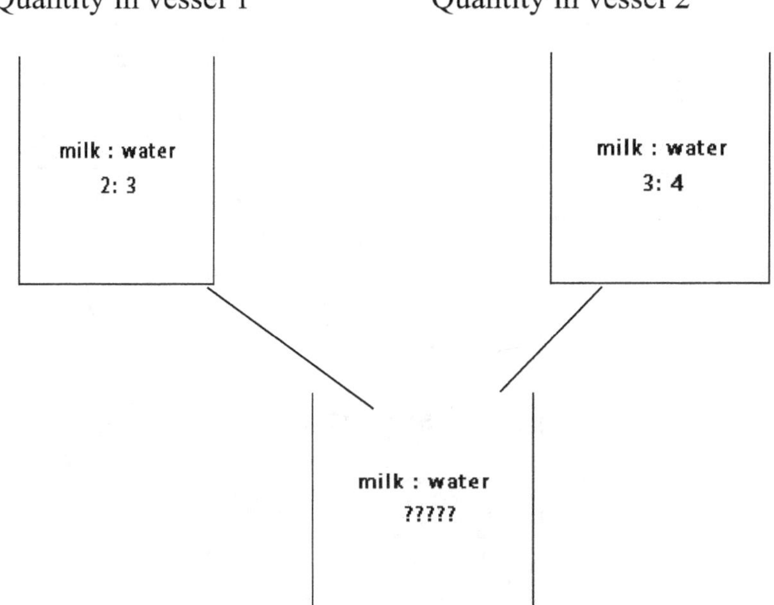

Here we know that both vessels are of equal size so let us take some value of mixture for both the vessels

2+3=5 parts 3+4=7 parts

(Let's take some quantity of mixture in both vessels.)

So for 5, 7 the suitable number is 35

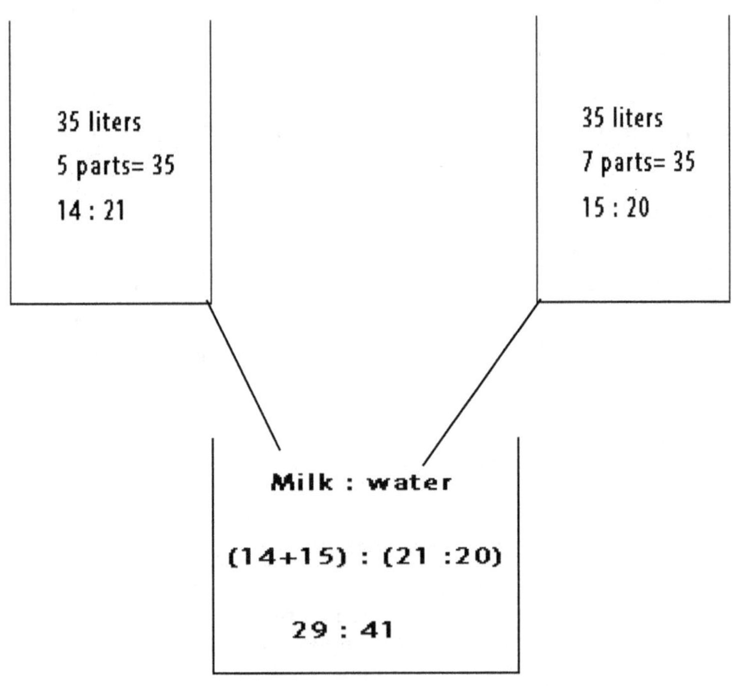

2. If the volume of the mixture in vessel 1 is twice the volume of the mixture in vessel 2. When both are mixed together than what is the ratio of m: w: s in resultant vessels?

Solution:

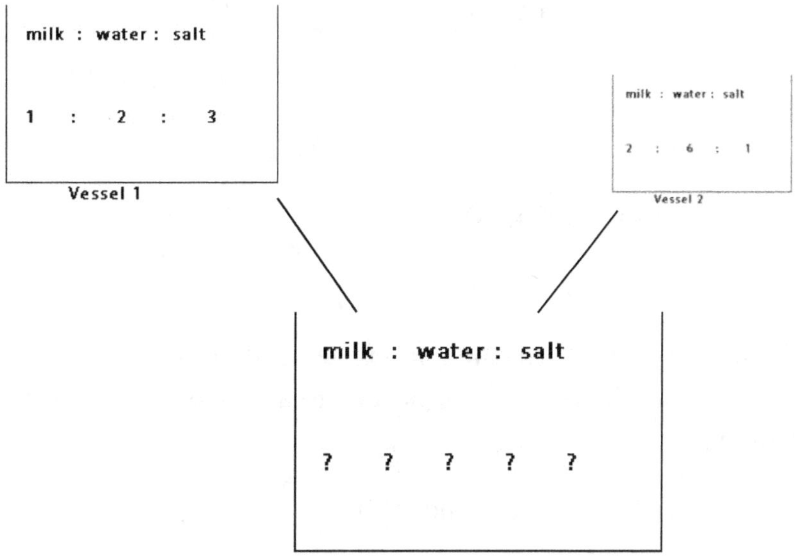

Let's try to take some quantity of mixture in both vessels

Vessel 1	=	m: w: s =	1: 2: 3	= 6 parts
Vessel 2	=	m: w: s =	2: 6: 1	= 9 parts

Given volume in V1 = 2 x volume in V2

Let V2 = 18

➔ $V_1 = 2(18) = 36$

➔ $V_1 = 36$

$V_1 = 36L$

$6p = 36L$

$1p = 6L$

m: w: s = 1: 2: 3

x x x

6L 6L 6L

6L 12L 18L

$V_2 = 18L$

$9p = 18L$

$1p = 2L$

m: w: s = 2: 6: 1

x x x

2L 2L 2L

4L 12L 2L

m: w: s = (6+4): (12+12): (18+2)

m: w: s = 10: 24: 20

m: w: s: = 5: 12: 10

3. In 80 liters mixture of milk and water, milk to water ratio is 4:1, how many liters of water needed to add in order to make the ratio as 1:4?

Solution: If 80 liters are in the ratio 4:1,

5 parts = 80 liters

1 parts = 16 liters

we can say 64 liters of milk and 16 liters of water

Let x liters of water be added to the mixture, so milk to water ratio will be 1:4.

$m{:}w \;=\; 64{:}(16+x) = 1{:}4$

$$=> \frac{64}{16+x} = \frac{1}{4}$$

$$=> 64 \times 4 = (16 + x) \times 1$$

$$=> 256 = 16 + x$$

$$=> x = 240\ liters$$

So 240 *liters of water needed to add inorder to make the mixture ratio as* 1:4.

b)Allegations:

A simpler way to solve the Mixtures questions we use allegations.

When can we use Allegations

1. When we mix only 2 varieties.
2. The value can be in percentages, ratios, numbers etc.
3. The resultant mixture value is in between the 1st value and 2nd value.
4. Always subtract lower number from higher number (Negative values are not allowed).

e) Examples:

1. A shopkeeper bought 2 varieties of sugar. Cost of first variety is \$30/kg and cost of second variety is \$50/kg. In what ratio should shopkeeper mix both the varieties so he can sell the resultant at a price of \$44/kg?

Sol: Mixture way

Let x kgs of variety 1 is mixed with y kgs of variety2

So total price of

$V_1 = x\ kgs \times \$30/kg = 30x.$

$V_2 = y\ kgs \times \$50/kg = 50y.$

$$Average\ Price = \frac{30x + 50y}{x + y} = \$44$$

$$30x + 50y = 44(x + y)$$

$$30x + 50y = 44x + 44y$$

$$50y - 44y = 44x - 30x$$

$$6y = 14x$$

$$\frac{6}{14} = \frac{x}{y}$$

$$x{:}y = 3{:}7$$

(We should mix both the varieties in the ratio 3:7)

Allegation way:

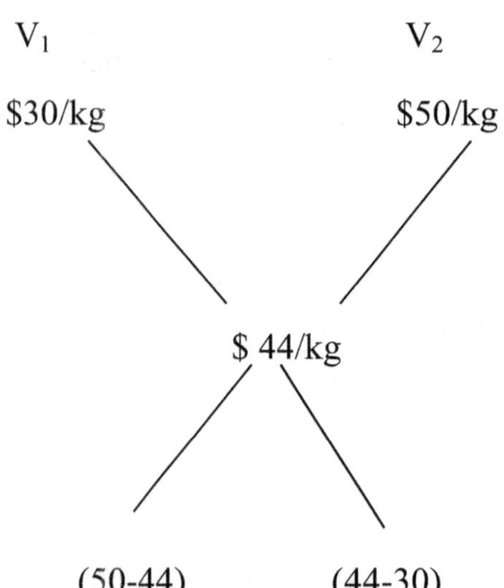

So rather than solving in mixtures way ,if we use allegations we can get the result easily.

2. Two vessels containing milk and water in the ratio 2:3 and 7:3. In what ratio both the vessels should be mixed so that the resultant vessel should contain milk to water in the ratio 1:1?

Solution:

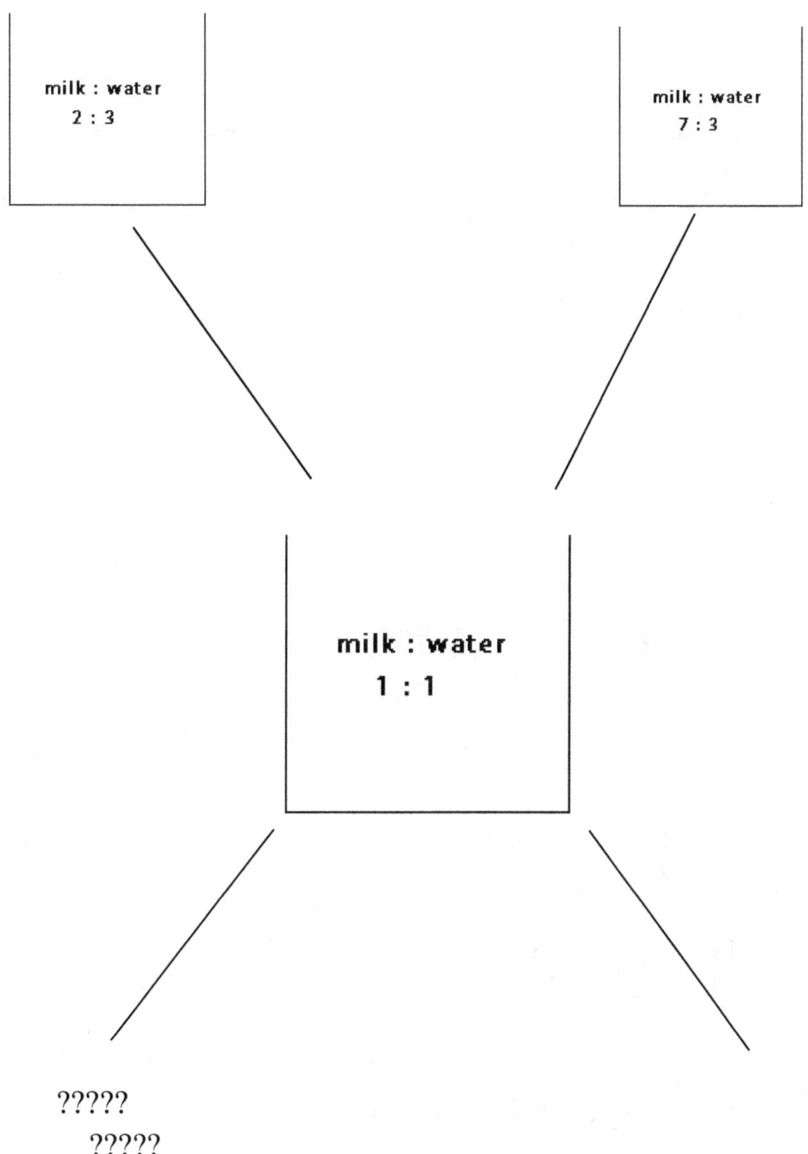

Method 1(using milk)

Method 2 (using water)

$V_1 \rightarrow m{:}w = 2{:}3$

$V_1 \rightarrow Fraction\ of\ milk = \frac{2}{5}$

$V_1 \rightarrow Fraction\ of\ water = \frac{3}{5}$

$V_2 \rightarrow m{:}w = 7{:}3$

$V_2 \rightarrow Fraction\ of\ milk = \frac{7}{10}$

$V_2 \rightarrow Fraction\ of\ water = \frac{3}{10}$

$V_1 + V_2 \rightarrow m{:}w = 1{:}1$

$V_1 + V_2 \rightarrow Fraction\ of\ milk = \frac{1}{2}$

$V_1 + V_2 \rightarrow Fraction\ o\ water = \frac{1}{2}$

V_1 V_2 V_1

V_2

2/5 7/10 3/5

3/10

½ ½

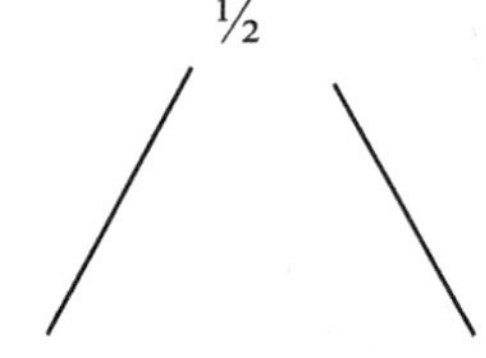

$\left(\frac{7}{10} - \frac{1}{2}\right) : \left(\frac{1}{2} - \frac{2}{5}\right)$

$\left(\frac{1}{2} - \frac{3}{10}\right) : \left(\frac{3}{5} - \frac{1}{2}\right)$

$\left(\frac{7-5}{10}\right) : \left(\frac{5-4}{10}\right)$

$\left(\frac{5-3}{10}\right) : \left(\frac{6-5}{10}\right)$

$$\frac{2}{10}:\frac{1}{10}$$

$$\frac{2}{10}:\frac{1}{10}$$

2: 1

2: 1

Method 3(using milk)

Method 4 (using water)

V_1 → m: w = 2: 3 = 5 parts, V_2 → m: w = 7: 3 = 10 parts

Let us take good numbers for 5 parts and 10 parts is "10"

In 'V1' 5 parts = 10

1 part = 2

V1 → Milk = 2*2 = 4 parts

V1 → Water =3*2 = 6 parts

V1+V2 → Milk = 1*5 = 5 parts

In 'V2'10 parts = 10

1 part = 1

V2 →Milk = 7*1 = 7 parts

V2 →Water = 3*1 = 3 parts

V1+V2 →Water = 1*5 = 5 parts

V_1 (milk) V_2 (milk) V_1 (water)

V_2 (water)

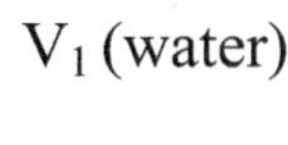

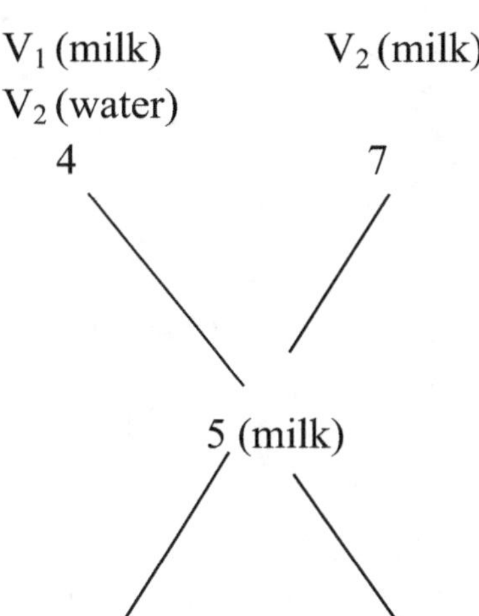

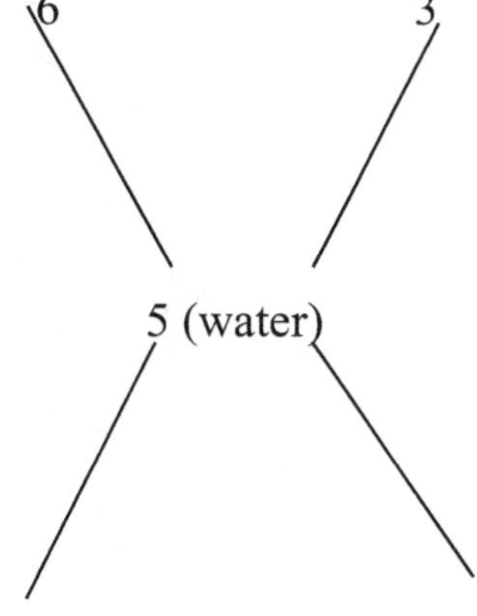

2 : 1 2 : 1

So we should mix both the vessels in the ratio 2:1

3. In a farm there are two types of animals Hens and Goats. A person observed that there are 40 eyes and 64 legs. Then find the total number of goats in the farm?

Solution:

It was given that there are 40 eyes means 20 animals

If all the animals are Hens = 20 x 2 = 40 legs

If all the animals are Goats = 20 x 4 = 80 legs

In question it was given as 64 legs

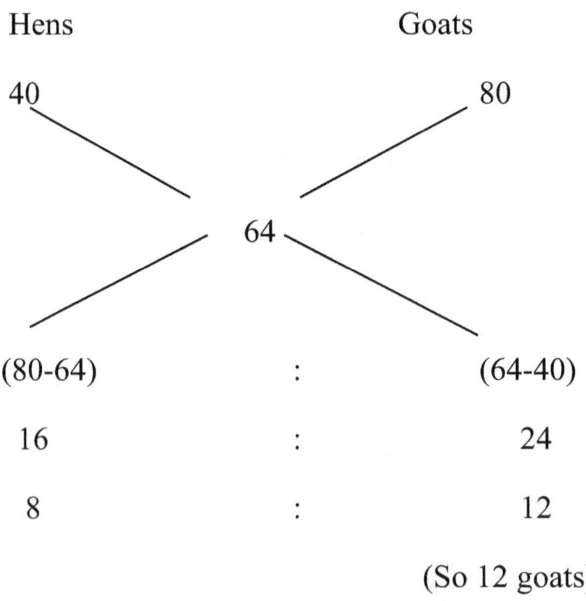

Time and Work

a) Model-1 (Based on proportions)

The relation between work,men,days and hours can be represented as follows

$Work\uparrow Men\uparrow$

$Work\uparrow Days\uparrow$

$work\uparrow Time\uparrow$

$$work \propto men$$

$work \propto days$

$work \propto hours$

$work \;\; \propto \;\; men \times days \times hours$

$$W = K \times M \times D \times H$$

(When remove proportion we put a constant)

$$\frac{W}{MDH} = K$$

$$\frac{W_1}{M_1D_1H_1} = \frac{W_2}{M_2D_2H_2}$$

Example 1:-

10 members can complete 3 buildings in 50 days by working 9 hours in a day. In how many days can 18 members build 9 similar types of building by working 6 hours a day?

Case1:

Men = 10

Case2:

Men= 18

Work = 3 | Work = 9

Days = 50 | Days = x

Time = 9 | Time = 6

$$So \quad \frac{W_1}{M_1D_1H_1} = \frac{W_2}{M_2D_2H_2}$$

$$\frac{3}{10 \times 50 \times 9} = \frac{9}{18 \times x \times 6}$$

$$=> x\ (No\ of\ required\ days) = 125$$

Example 2:-

5 Monkeys can eat 5 bananas in 5 days. How many Monkeys are required to eat 55 bananas in 55 days?

$M_1 = 5$ | $M_2 = x$

$W_1 = 5$ | $W_2 = 55$

$D_1 = 5$ | $D_2 = 55$

$$\frac{W_1}{M_1D_1H_1} = \frac{W_2}{M_2D_2H_2}$$

$$\frac{5}{5 \times 5} = \frac{55}{x \times 55}$$

$$x = 5$$

(So 5 monkeys are required to eat 55 bananas in 55 days).

Model-2 (Unitary method):

Example1:-

'A' can complete a task in 10 days. 'B' can complete the same task in 15 days and 'C' can complete the same task in 30 days. In how many days can A, B, C all together complete the task.

Solution 1:-

A = 10 Days B = 15 Days C = 30 Days

Let us take a value for our task

In this case the best value is multiple of 10, 15 and 30. The numbers are 30, 60, 90…..

(Pick any number you like)

Let my task here is eating 60 chocolates

$A(1) = \frac{60}{10} = 6$ (In one day A can eat 6 Choclates)

$B(1) = \frac{60}{15} = 4$ (In one day B can eat 4 Choclates)

$C(1) = \frac{60}{30} = 2$ (In one day C can eat 2 Choclates)

A+B+C (1) = 6+4+2 = 12 (In one day A,B and C together can eat 12 chocolates)

$$so,\ A,B\ and\ C\ can\ eat\ 60\ chocolates\ in\ \frac{60}{12} = 5\ Days$$

Solution 2:-

A → 10 → 3 Units

B → 15 30 → 2 Units

C → 30 → 1 Units

$$= \frac{30}{3+2+1} = \frac{30}{6} = 5\ days$$

Example2:-

A can complete a task in 20 days. B can complete the same task in 30 days. If A worked for 8 days and left the job, in how many days 'B' alone can complete the remaining work?

Solution:-

A = 20 days B = 30 days

A worked for = 8 days B worked for =?

Here total work done by both the people can be taken as 1.

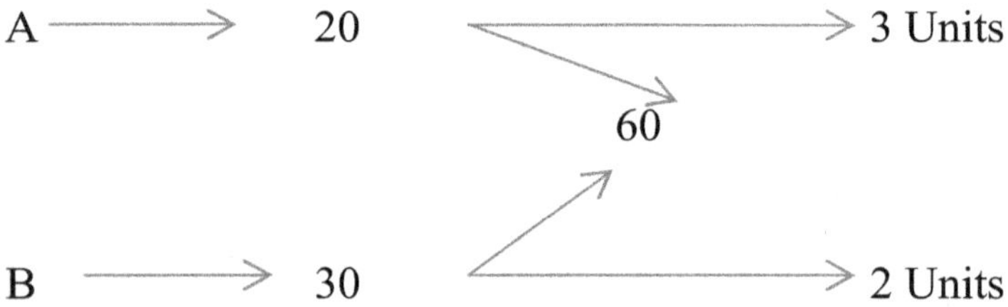

A completed = 8 days × 3 units = 24 Units

Remaining Work = 60 Units – 24 Units = 36 Units

Number of days required for B = 36/2 =18 days

So 'B' requires 18 days to complete the remaining work.

Model 3 (Total work is always '1'):

Here a1,a2,a3 → Total number of days required to complete the work.

x1,x2,x3 → Number of days actually worked by the people.

$$\frac{x_1}{a_1} + \frac{x_2}{a_2} + \frac{x_3}{a_3} + \dots = 1$$

Example:-

A, B and C can complete a task in 10 days, 20 days and 30 days respectively. All three together started the task and worked for 2 days then 'C' left the job. A & B worked for 2 days then 'C' replaced 'A' and C & B worked for 2 days, 'B' left the job in how many days 'C' can complete the remaining job?

Solution 1:-

A = 10 days B = 20 Days C = 30 days

A + B + C = 2 days

A + B = 2 days

B + C = 2 days

C = ?0

A	→	10		→ 6 Units
B	→	20	60	→ 3 Units
C	→	30		→ 2 Units

A+B+C (1) =	6+3+2 =	11x 2 =	22 Units
A + B (1) =	6 + 3 =	9 x 2 =	18 Units
B + C (1) =	3 + 2 =	5 x 2 =	10 Units

Completed Work = 50 Units

Remaining Work = 60 – 50 = 10 Units

In 1 day 'C' can do '2' Units.

$$So, C\ can\ complete\ the\ remaining\ work\ in\ \frac{10}{2} = 5\ days$$

Solution 2:

A = 10 days B = 20 Days C = 30 days

A + B + C = 2 days

A + B = 2 days

B + C = 2 days

C = x

Totally 'A' worked for = 4 days

'B' worked for = 6 days

'C' worked for = 4 + x days

$$\frac{x_1}{a_1}+\frac{x_2}{a_2}+\frac{x_3}{a_3}=1$$

$$\frac{4}{10}+\frac{6}{20}+\frac{(4+x)}{30}=1$$

$$\frac{4}{10}\times\frac{6}{6}+\frac{6}{20}\times\frac{3}{3}+\frac{(4+x)}{30}\times\frac{2}{2}=1$$

$$\frac{24}{60}+\frac{18}{60}+\frac{8+2x}{60}=1$$

$$\frac{24+18+8+2x}{60}=1$$

$$50+2x=60$$

$$2x=60-50$$

$$2x=10$$

$$x=5\ days$$

So 'C' requires 5 days to complete the remaining work.

Model -4 (Based on capacities):

Example 1: Capacity of 'A' is twice the capacity of 'B' and capacity of 'B' is thrice the capacity of 'C'. If all the three together can complete a task in 6 days, in how many days 'B' alone can complete the task.

A's capacity = 2(B's Capacity)

B's capacity = 3(C's Capacity)

Let C can do 1 unit of work in a day

C = 1 Units

B = 1 x 3 = 3 Units

A = 2 x 3 = 6 Units

A + B + C (1) = 6 + 3 + 1 = 10 Units

So A,B,C worked for 6days to complete the task so the total work is 60 Units

B alone can complete the work = 60/3 = 20 days.

Model- 5 (Pipes and Cisterns):

Example 1: A tank has two filling taps A, B. Water flows at 10 lit/hr and 20 lit/hr and one leak 'C' empties the tank at a rate of 15lit/hr. In how much time a tank of 150 liters capacity will be filled.

Solution:-

A = 10lit/hr B = 20lit/hr C = -15lit/hr

A + B + C (1hr) = 10 + 20 – 15 = 15 lit/hr

$$tank\ will\ be\ filled\ in = \frac{150lit}{15lit/hr} = 10hours$$

Example 2: A tank has two filling taps A, B. Tap A can fill the tank in 10 hrs, Tap B can fill the tank in 20hrs and one leak 'C' empties the tank in 15 hrs. In how much time the tank will be filled?

Solution:-

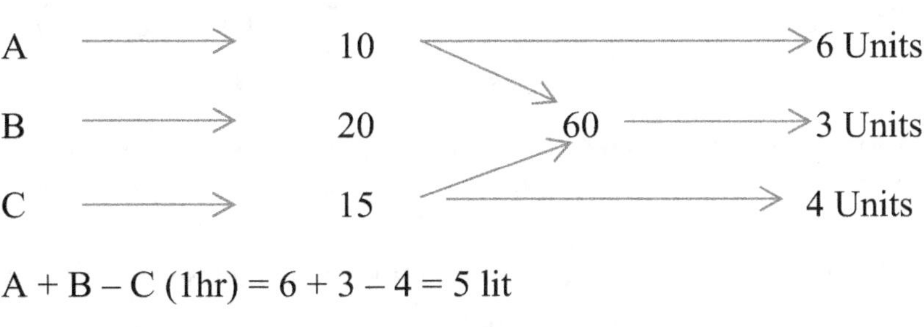

A + B – C (1hr) = 6 + 3 – 4 = 5 lit

So to fill complete tank = $\frac{60}{5} = 12\ hours$

Example 3: A tank has filling taps A, B and emptying tap C . Tap A can fill the tank in 5 hours and Tap B can fill the tank in10 hours and Tap C can empty the tank in 30 hours, if all three taps work on alternate hours starting with Tap 'A' then 'B' and 'C'. In how many hours the tank will be filled?

Solution: Let us take the Capacity of tank be Multiple of 5,10 and 30 which is equal to 30 Units

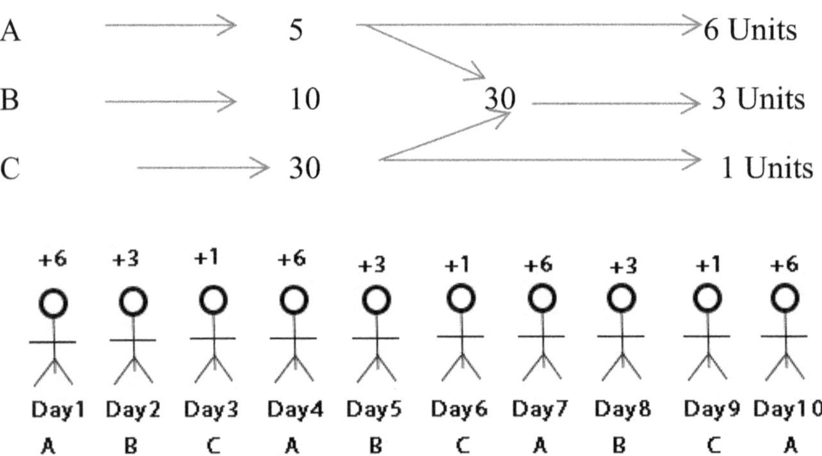

So, All 3 taps can fill the complete tank in 10 hours by working on alternate hours.

Time, Speed and Distance

The three types of questions what we find in Time and Work topic are

$$a)\ Speed = \frac{Distance}{Time}$$

$$b)\ Average\ Speed = \frac{Total\ Distance\ travelled}{Total\ Time\ taken}$$

$$c)\ Relative\ Speed = \frac{S1 + S2(opposite\ direction)}{}$$

3 m/sec **2 m/sec**

$$R.S = S1 + S2$$

$$R.S = 3\ +\ 2 = 5\ m/sec$$

$$Relative\ Speed = \frac{S1 - S2(Same\ direction)}{}$$

3 m/sec **2 m/sec**

$$R.S = S1 - S2$$

$$R.S = 3 - 2 = 1\ m/sec$$

Relative Speed (Example Problems):

1. A thief snatches a chain and moves with a speed of 30 miles/hours, after 5 hours police arrives the place and starts chasing the thief at the speed of 35 miles/hour. In how much time will the police catch the thief?

35miles/hour

30miles/hour

Solution:

Here in 5 Hours thief travels for a distance of 150 Miles.

Distance between Police and thief = 150 Miles.

And Police is Chasing the thief so they are moving in the same direction so Relative speed is S1-S2

Relative Speed = 35-30 =5 Miles/hour.

$$Time = \frac{Distance}{Relative\ Speed} = \frac{150}{5} = 30\ hour$$

2. A train starts from station A to station B at 6 o'clock in the morning with a speed of 60 miles per hour after 4 hours another train started from station B to Station A with a speed of 80 miles per hour. If the distance between both the stations is 1010 miles, at what time will both the trains meet each other and what is the distance to the meeting point from station B?

Solution:

Here for first 4 hours from 6'o clock to 10'o clock Train1 travels= 4 *60 =240 Miles

So the distance between both trains at 10'o clock = 1010 miles – 240 miles = 770 Miles

Both trains are moving in the same direction so relative speed = 60 + 80 = 140 Miles/hour

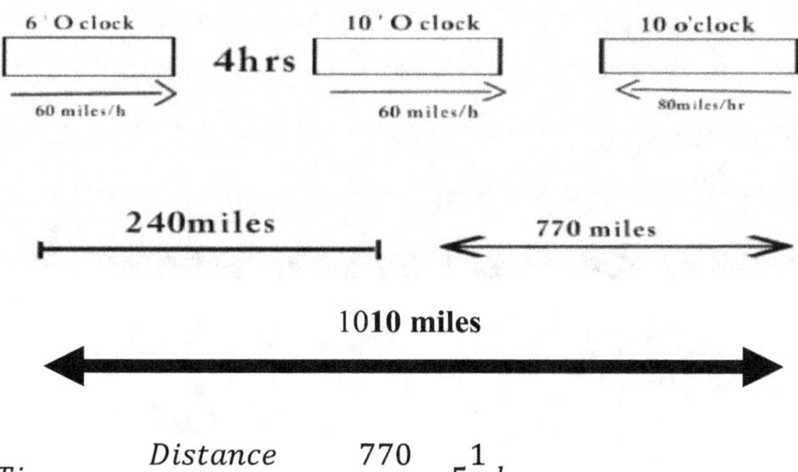

$$Time = \frac{Distance}{Reletive\ Speed} = \frac{770}{140} = 5\frac{1}{2}\ hrs$$

So both trains meet after

$5\frac{1}{2}$ *hrs from* 10'*oclock* . *So both the trains meet*

at 15:30 *Hours*

$$Distance\ travel\ from\ station\ B = 5\frac{1}{2}\ hrs \times 80 = 440\ miles$$

(Since train B starts only at 10'o clock).

Average Speed (Example Problem):

3. A person travels from "x" to "y" at the speed of 40 miles/hr and return from y to x at the speed of 50 miles/hour and again travels from "x" to "y" at the speed of 60miles/hour. Find the average speed of the total journey?

Solution: Let us take a value for the distance between 'x' and 'y'

The best value is Multiple of 40,50 and 60 = 600 Miles

So the total distance travelled = 3*600 Miles = 1800 Miles.

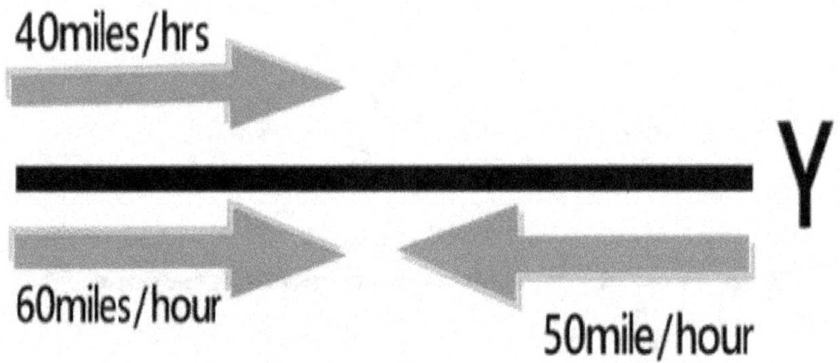

$$Average\ Speed = \frac{Total\ Distance}{Total\ Time}$$

$$Average\ Speed = \frac{1800}{(\frac{600}{40} + \frac{600}{50} + \frac{600}{60})}$$

$$Average\ Speed = \frac{1800}{15 + 12 + 10}$$

$$Average\ Speed = \frac{1800}{37}\ miles/hours$$

<u>Speed (Example problem)</u>:

4. A person travels from his house to his office with a speed of 20 meters per second and reaches his house 6 seconds late than his usual time. If the same person travels with a speed of 30 meters per second, he will reach his home 4 seconds earlier. Find the distance, normal speed and normal time taken by the person?

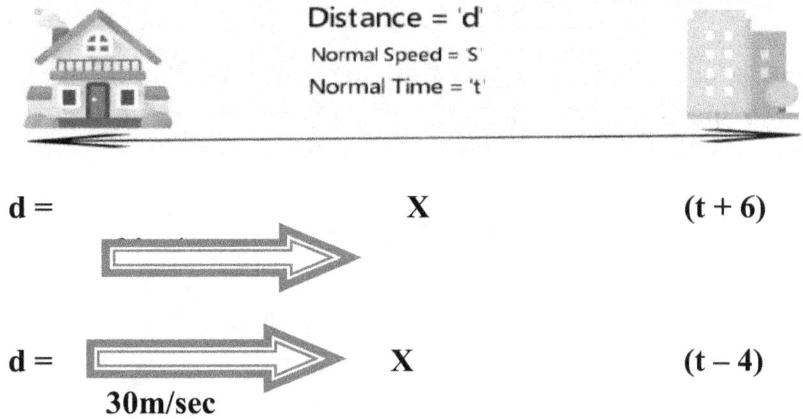

Here in both the cases distance between house and office is constant so we can equate both

$$Speed = \frac{Distance}{Time}$$

Distance = Speed * Time

$=> d = 20(t + 6) = 30(t - 4)$

$=> 20t + 120 = 30t - 120$

$=> 120 + 120 = 30t - 20t$

$=> 240 = 10t$

$=> 240/10 = t$

$=> t = 24\ seconds$

So 24 Seconds is the Normal time taken by the person to reach from his house to office.

So Distance = 20(24+6) = 30(24-4) = 600 meters

$$Speed = \frac{distance}{time} = \frac{600}{24} = 25m/s$$

So these are the different types of questions you can find in Time , Speed and Distance.

GEOMETRY

Geometry

Topics we discuss

1. Lines and Angles

2. Triangles

3. Quadrilaterals

4. Polygons

5. Circles

6. 3. D Geometry

7. Co-ordinate Geometry

1. Lines and Angles

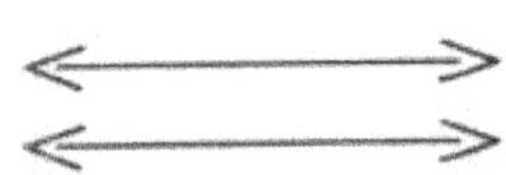

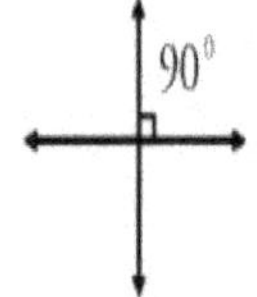

Parallel lines
(will not intersect)

Prependicular Lines
(Angle between them is
90^0)

Supplementary, Complimentary and Vertical Opposite Angles

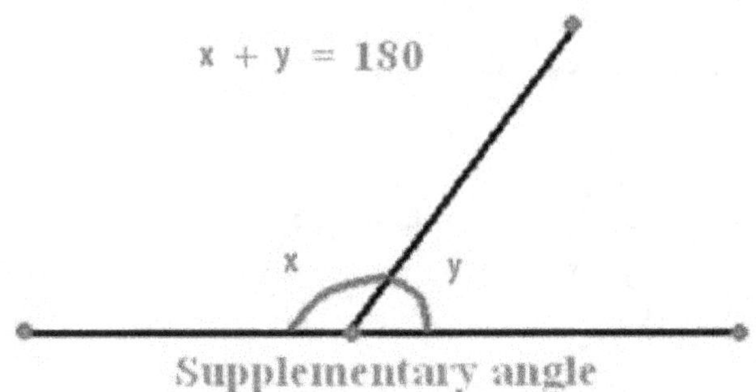

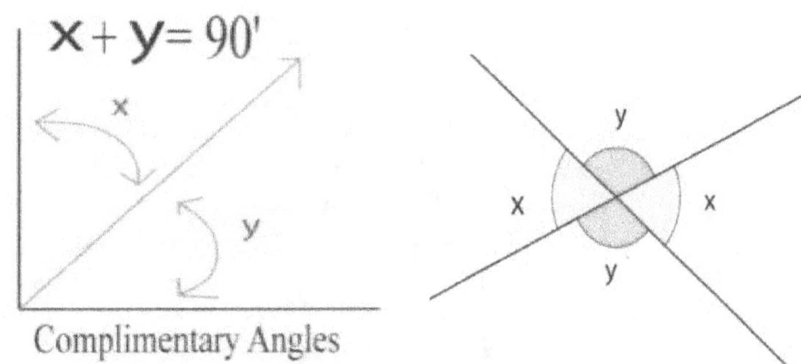

For two intersecting lines vertical opposite Angles are always equal

Parallel Lines

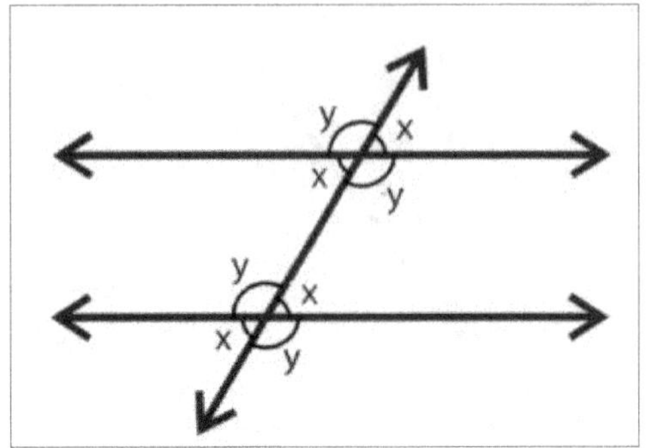

For two parallel lines if we draw a transversal (a line touching both the lines) we get 8 angles all small angels are equal and big angles are equal.

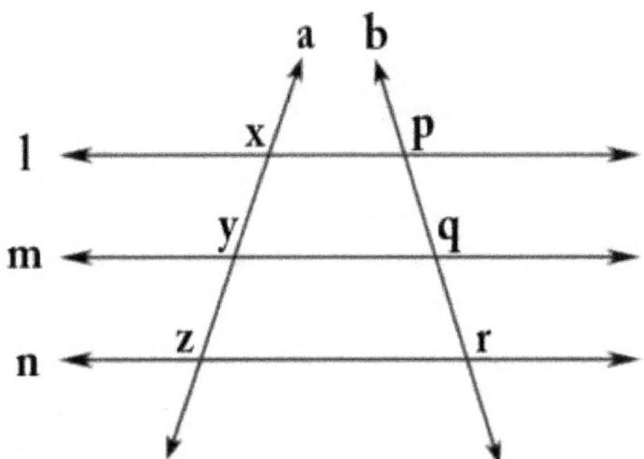

l, m, n are parallel lines a, b are two lines touching the parallel lines are divided in propotional.

$$\frac{xy}{yz}=\frac{pq}{qr}$$

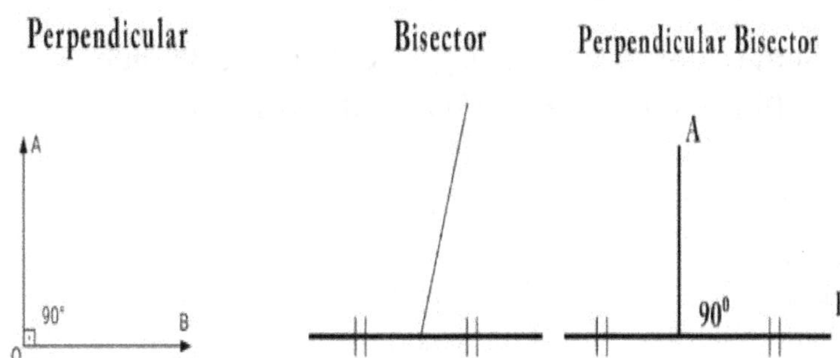

2. Triangles

1.

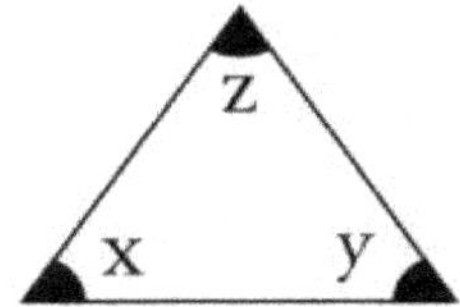

(Sum of angle in triangle is 180^0)

$x + y + z = 180'$

2.

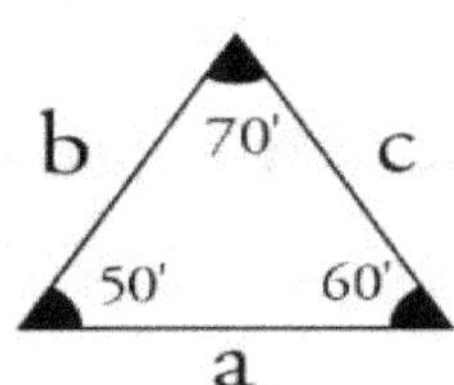

(The side opposite to largest angle will be longest side)

$a > b > c$

3. Basic properties to form a Triangle

1. Sum of any two sides is greater than the 3rd side
2. Difference between any two sides is less than the 3rd side

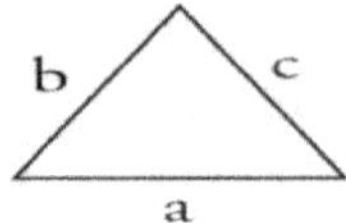

Difference between 1st and 2nd side < 3rd side < sum of 1st and 2nd side

Example:-

If 4 and 5 are two sides of triangle what are the possible values for the third side of the triangle?

$5 - 4 < third\ side < 5 + 4$

1 < third side < 9

4.Exterior Angles

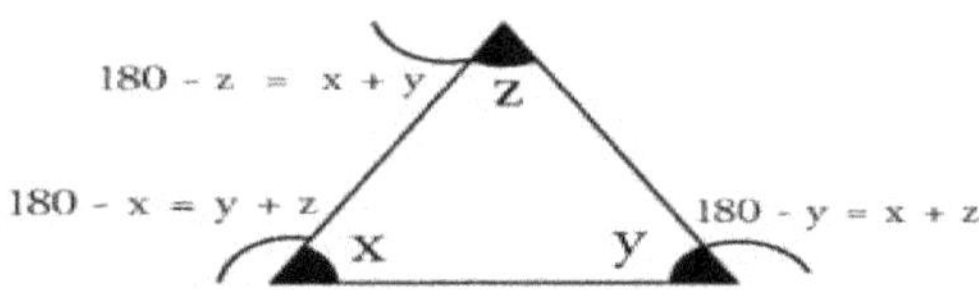

Each exterior angles = Sum of opposite Interior angles

$$Exterior\ of < y = \ < x + \ < z$$

$$Sum\ of\ Exterior\ angles = 180 - x + 180 - y + 180 - z$$

$$= 540 - (x + y + z)$$

$$= 540 - 180$$

$$= 360.$$

(or)

$$Sum\ of\ Exterior\ angles = x + y + y + z + z + x$$

$$= 2(x + y + z)$$

$$= 2(180)$$

$$= 360$$

5. <u>**Area of Triangle**</u>

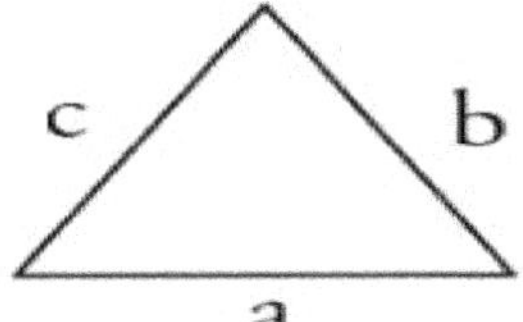

$$Area = \sqrt{s(s-a)(s-b)(s-c)} \quad \text{Where } S = \frac{a+b+c}{2}$$

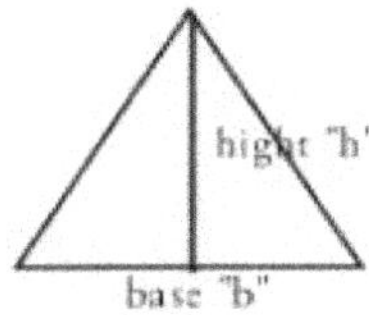

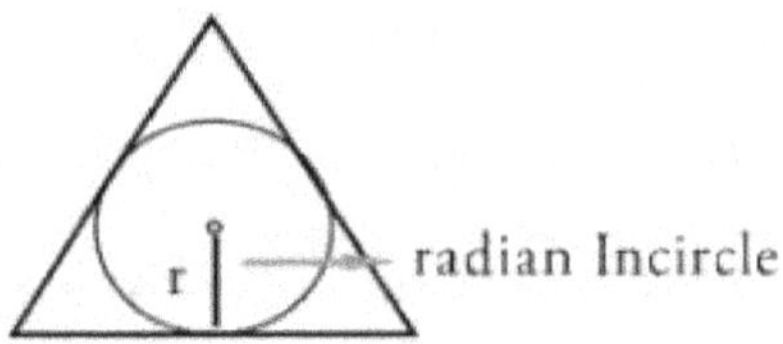

$Area = r.S$ $\quad$ $Where\ S = \dfrac{a+b+c}{2}$

6. Pythagorean Theorm

$(hpy)^2 = a^2 + b^2$

$c^2 = a^2 + b^2$

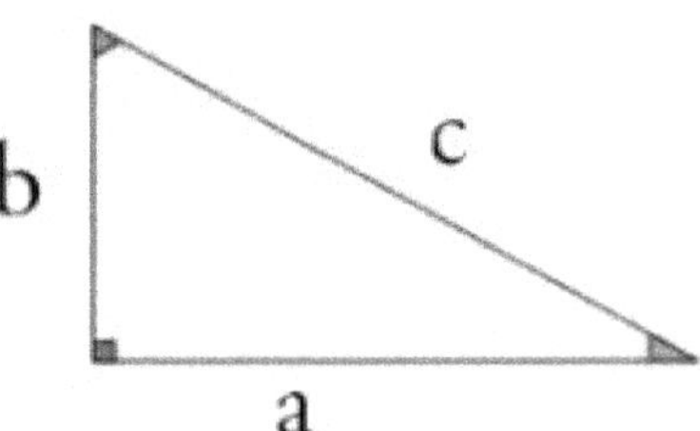

Equilateral Triangle

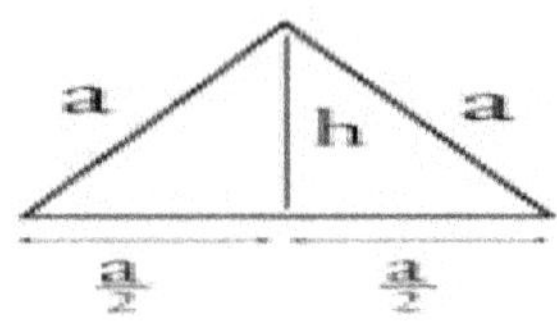

$a^2 = h^2 + (\frac{a}{2})^2 \quad => \quad h^2 = a^2 - \frac{a_2}{4}$

$$h^2 = \frac{4a^2 - a^2}{4} = \frac{3a^2}{4}$$

$$h = \frac{\sqrt{3}}{2}a$$

$$Area\ of\ Equilateral\ Triangle = \frac{1}{2} \times Base\ \times Height$$

$$Area\ of\ Equilateral\ Triangle = \frac{1}{2} \times a\ \times \frac{\sqrt{3}}{2}a$$

$$Area\ of\ Equilateral\ Triangle = \frac{\sqrt{3}}{4}a^2$$

7. Pythagorean Triplets

Two main triplets we commonly come across

1. 3, 4, 5 → 6, 8, 10 | 9, 12, 15 | $\frac{3}{2}, \frac{4}{2}, \frac{5}{2}$
2. 5, 12, 13 → 10, 24, 26 | 15, 36, 39 | $\frac{5}{2}, \frac{12}{2}, \frac{13}{2}$

(The entire triangle formed in this ratio forms the Pythagorean triples)

8. Similar Triangles

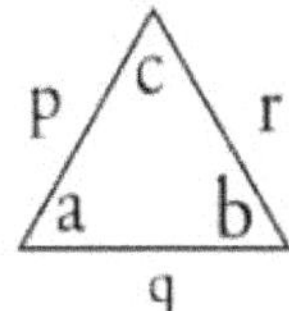

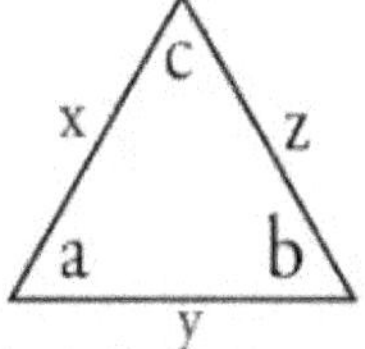

(The angles in two triangles are same and ratios of sides are in proportion)

$$\frac{p}{x}=\frac{q}{y}=\frac{r}{z}$$

Congruent Triangles

Two triangles with same shape and size are called as congruent triangles

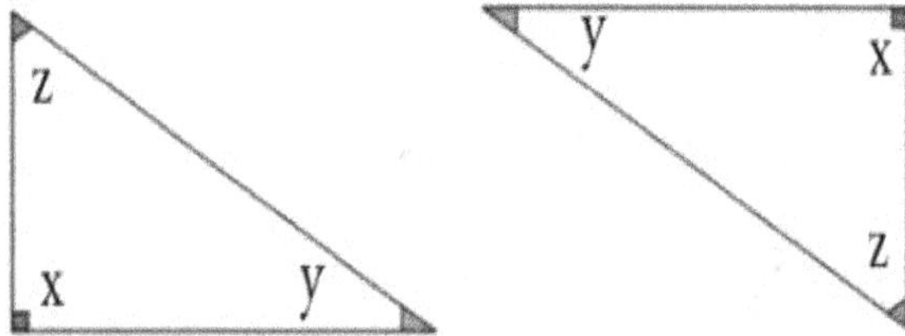

9. Types of Triangles

Scalene Triangle

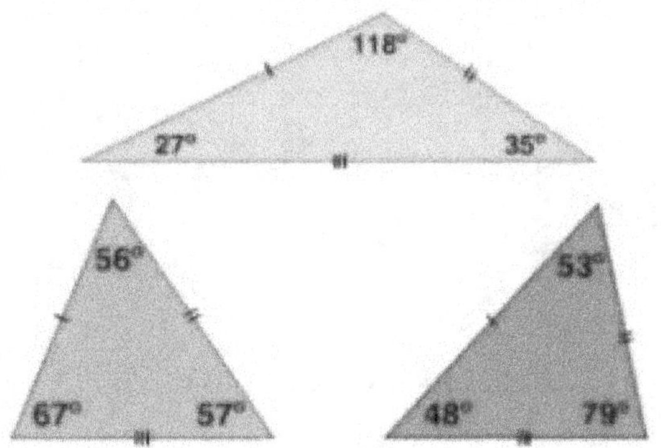

No Equal angles and sides

Right Angle Triangle

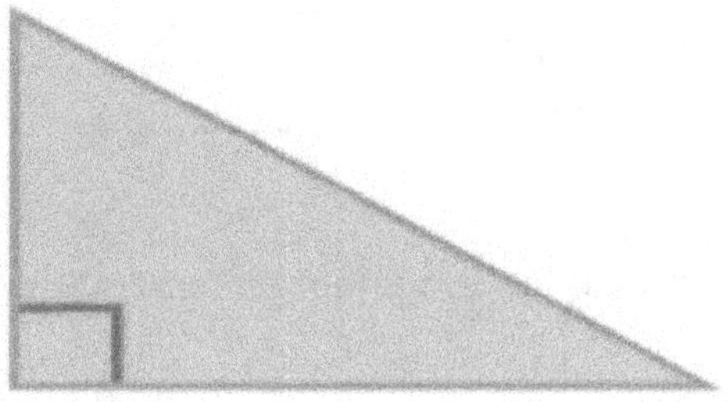

One angle is 90^0

Acute triangle

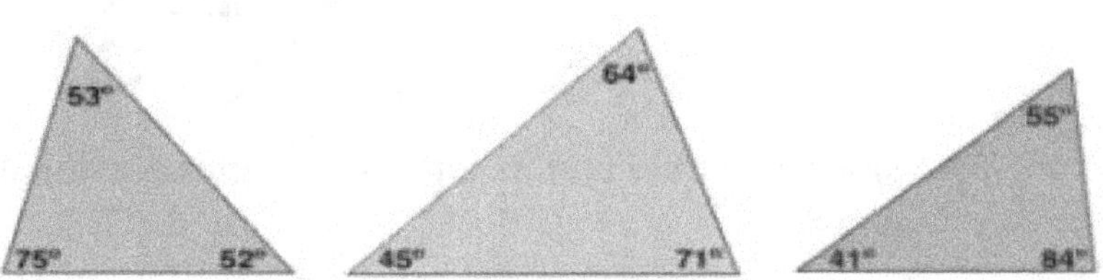

Three angles are less than 90^0

Obtuse triangle

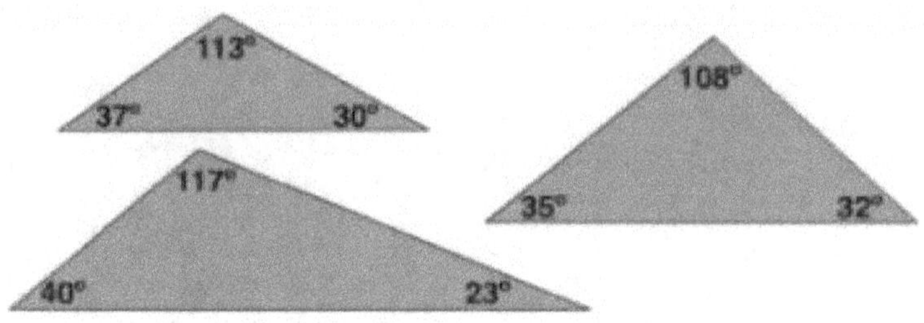

One angle is greater than 90^0

Equilateral Triangle

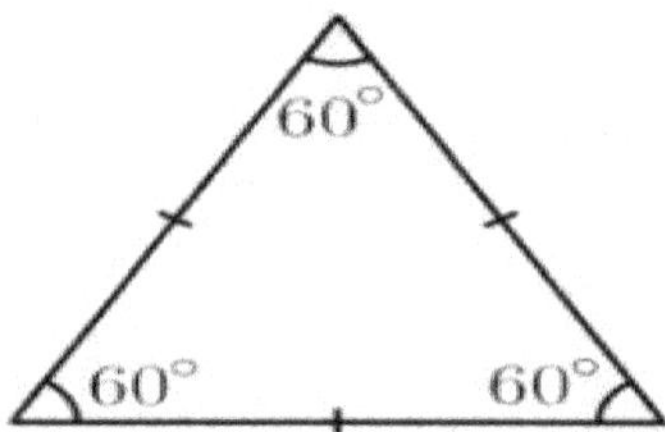

All sides are equal and all angles are equal to 60^0

Isosceles Triangle

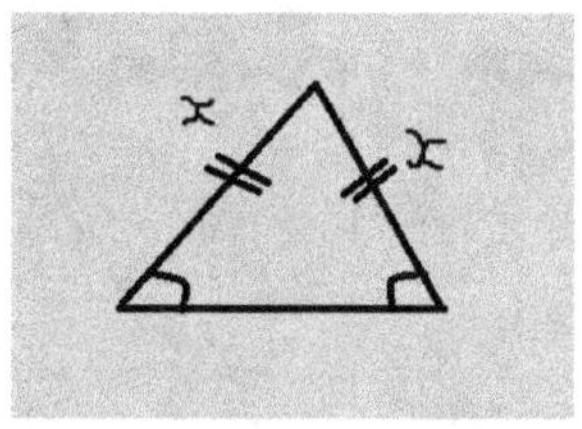

Two sides are equal and its Opposite angles are equal

Isosceles Right angle Triangle

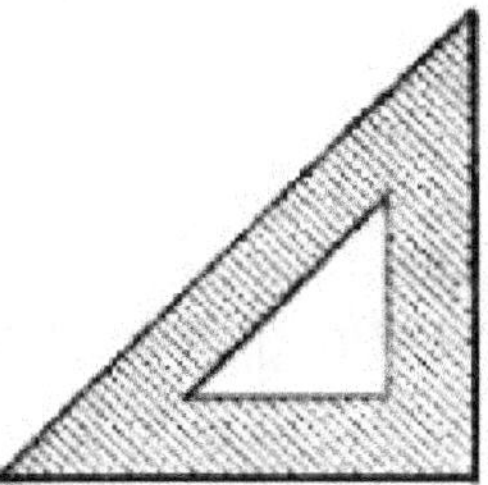

Two sides and two angles are equal and angles are 45', 45' and 90'

10. **Centers**

a) In center

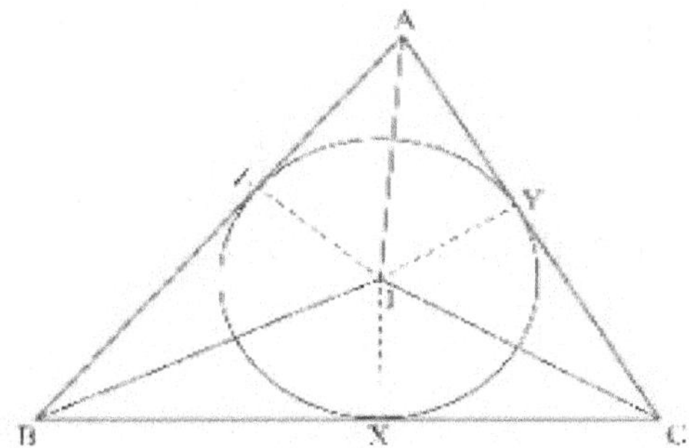

Points of intersection of angular bisectors is called as Incenter

b) Circumcenter

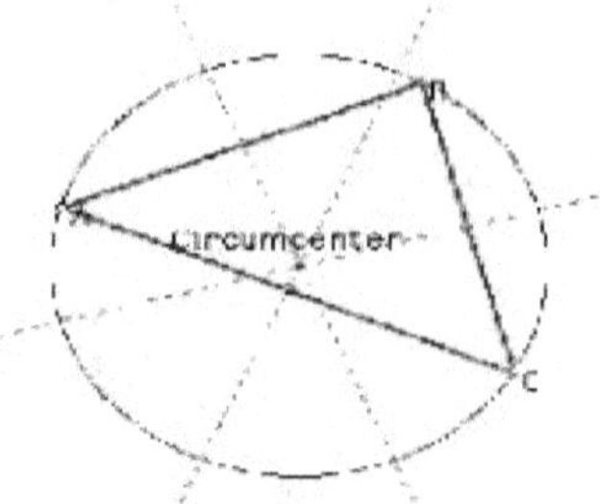

Points of intersection of perpendicular bisectors of sides is called as Circumcenter

c) Ex center

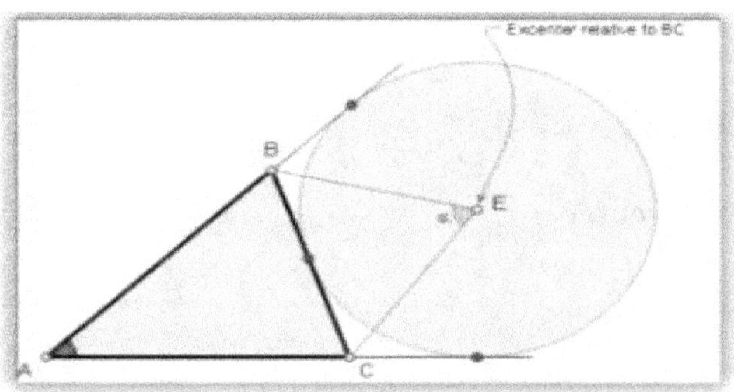

Points of intersection of one internal bisector and two external bisectors

d) Centroid

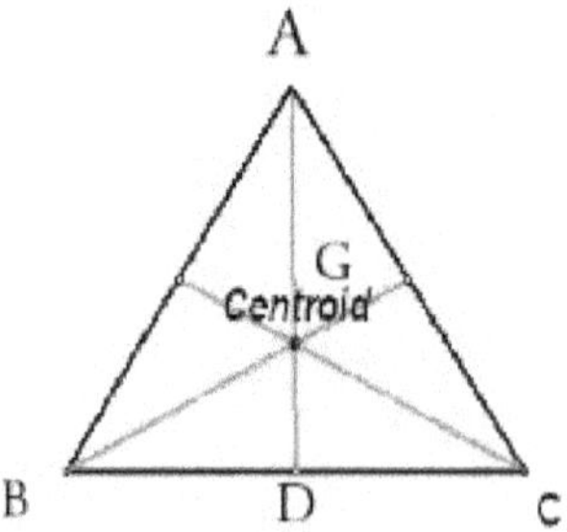

Points of intersection of Medians is Centroid divides the median in the ratio 2:1

e) Ortho Center

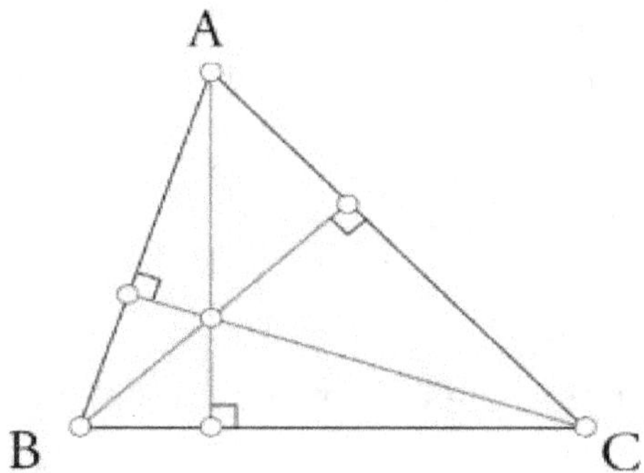

The Point of intersection of Perpendicular

f) Mid-point theorem

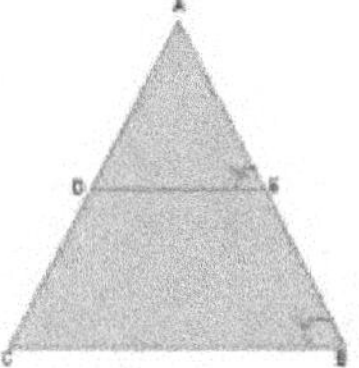

The line joining Mid-points of any two sides is parallel to side 3rd and half of the 3rd side.

$Here\ DE = \frac{1}{2}(BC)$

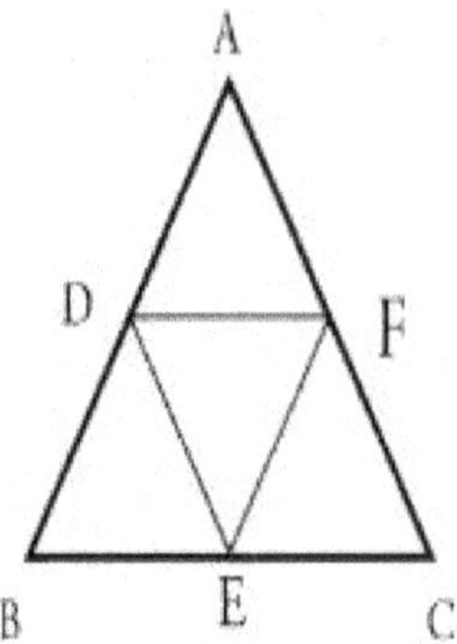

The Area of triangle formed by joining mid-points of triangle

$$Area\ of\ triangle\ DEF = \frac{1}{4}(Area\ of\ triangle\ ABC)$$

$$Perimeter\ of\ triangle\ DEF = \frac{1}{2}(Perimeter\ of\ triangle\ ABC)$$

Special Triangles

(i) 30, 60, 90

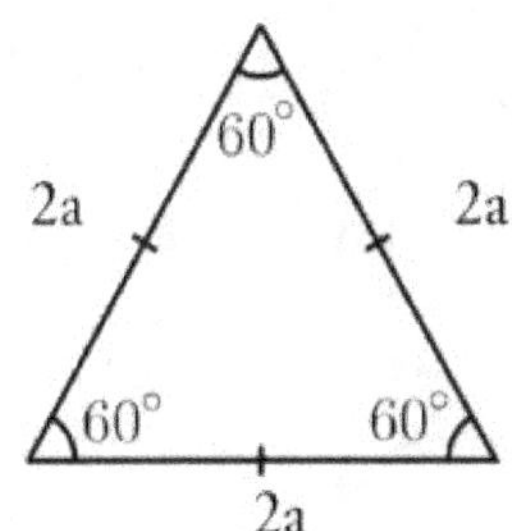

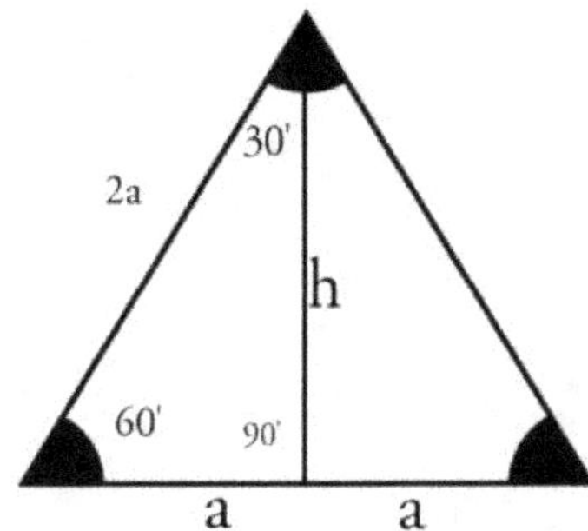

$$(2a)^2 = h^2 + a^2$$
$$4a^2 = h^2 + a^2$$
$$3a^2 = h^2$$
$$\sqrt{3}a = h$$

$\text{Length of side opposite to } 30' \to a$

$\text{Length of side opposite to } 60' \to \sqrt{3}a$

$\text{Length of side opposite to } 90' \to 2a$

$30' : 60' : 90' \to a : \sqrt{3}a : 2a$

$30' : 60' : 90' \to 1 : \sqrt{3} : 2 \ (sides\ ratio)$

(ii) 45’, 45’, 90’

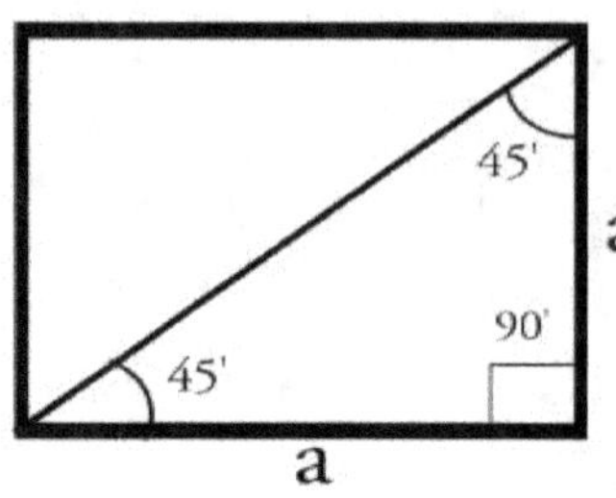

$$h^2 = a^2 + a^2$$

$$h^2 = 2a^2$$
$$h^2 = \sqrt{2}a$$

$Length\ of\ side\ opposite\ to\ 45^{'} \quad \rightarrow\ a$

$Length\ of\ side\ opposite\ to\ 45^{'} \quad \rightarrow\ a$

$Length\ of\ side\ opposite\ to 90^{'} \quad \rightarrow \sqrt{2}\ a$

$45^{'}\ :\ 45^{'}\ :\ 90^{'} \rightarrow \quad a\ :\ a\ :\ \sqrt{2}a$

$45^{'}\ :\ 45^{'}\ :\ 90^{'} \rightarrow \quad 1\ :\ 1\ :\ \sqrt{2}$ (sides ratio)

Quadrilaterals

Sum of interior angles in quadrilateral = 360'

Sum of exterior angles in quadrilateral = 360'

1. Types of Quadrilateral

   a) Parallelogram

   b) Square

   c) Rectangle

   d) Rhombus

   e) Trapezium

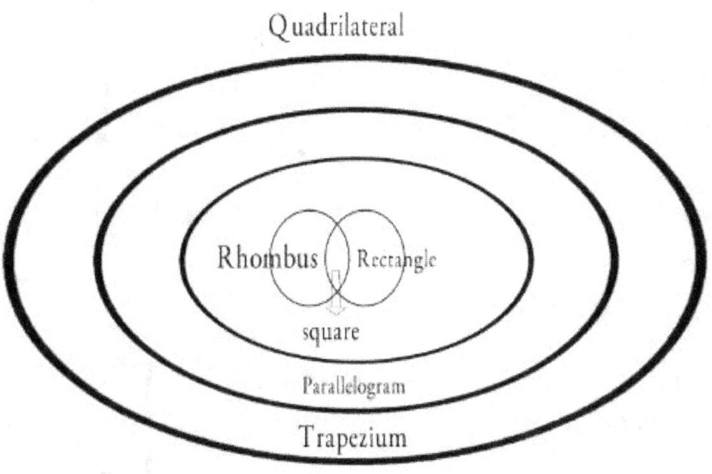

a) Parallelogram

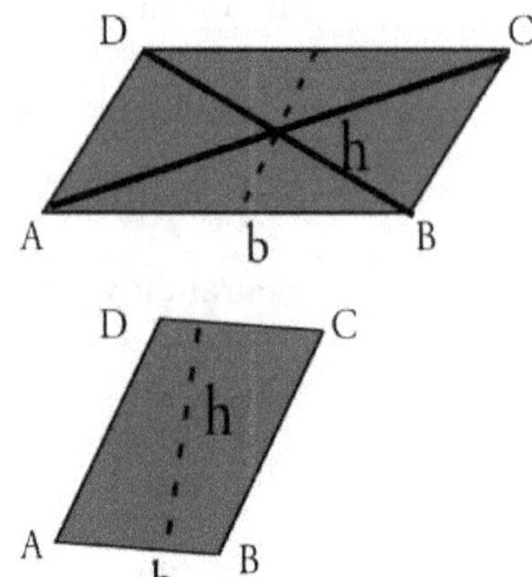

Opposite angles are equal

Opposite sides are equal

Adjacent angles sum is 180'

Diagonal bisect each other

$Area = base \times Height$

$perimeter = Sum\ of\ all\ sides$

b) Square

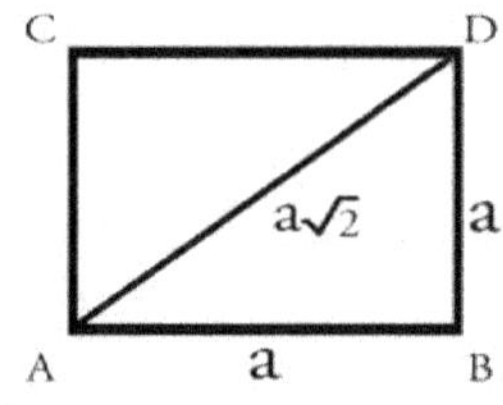

A parllelogram with all sides are equal and diagonal bisect eachother

$Area = a^2$

$$Area = \frac{1}{2} \times d^2$$

$Perimeter = 4a$

c) Rectangle

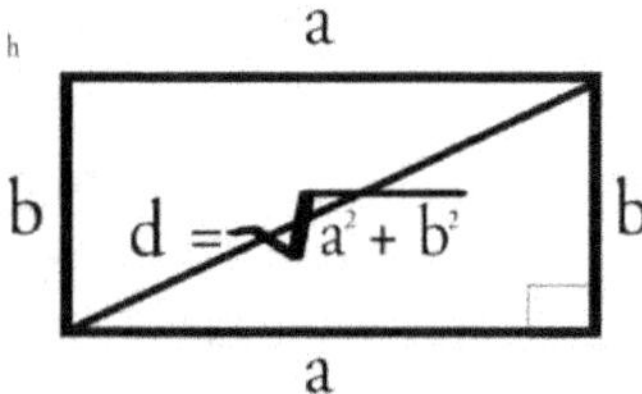

A parallelogram whose 4 angles are 90' and diagonals are equal in length.

$Area = a \times b$

$Perimeter = 2(a + b)$

d) Rhombus

A parallelogram whose 4 sides are equal and diagonals are bisect at 90’

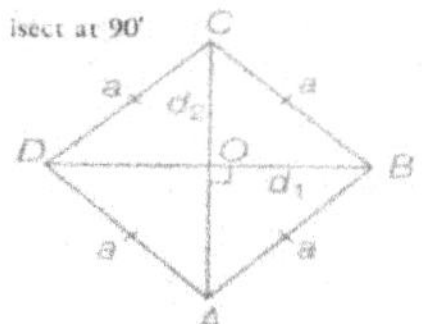

$$Area = \frac{1}{2} \times d1 \times d2$$

$$Perimeter = 4a$$

e) Trapezium

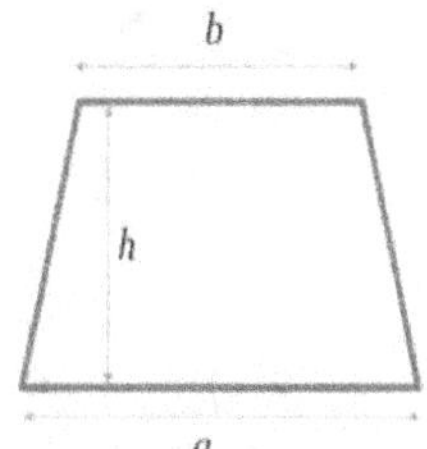

$$Area = \frac{1}{2}h(a + b)$$

$$Perimeter = Sum\ of\ all\ side$$

Quadrilateral

Any 4 side figure in Quadrilateral

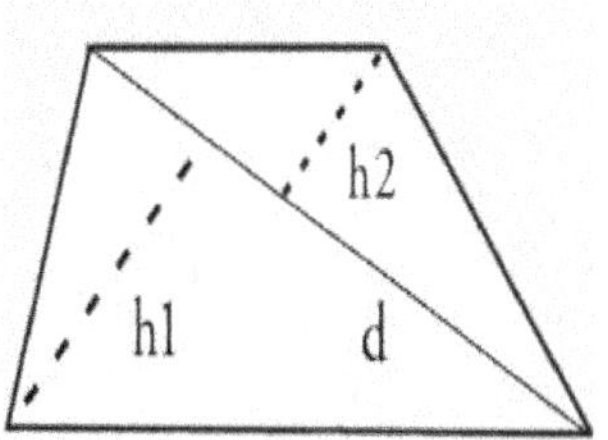

$$Area = \frac{1}{2}d(h1 + h2)$$

$$Perimeter = Sum\ of\ sides$$

Polygons

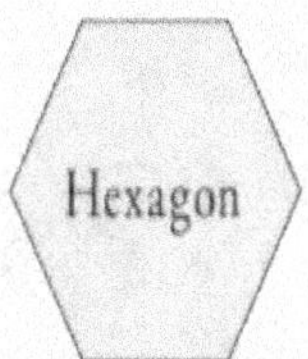

1) Sum of Interior angle

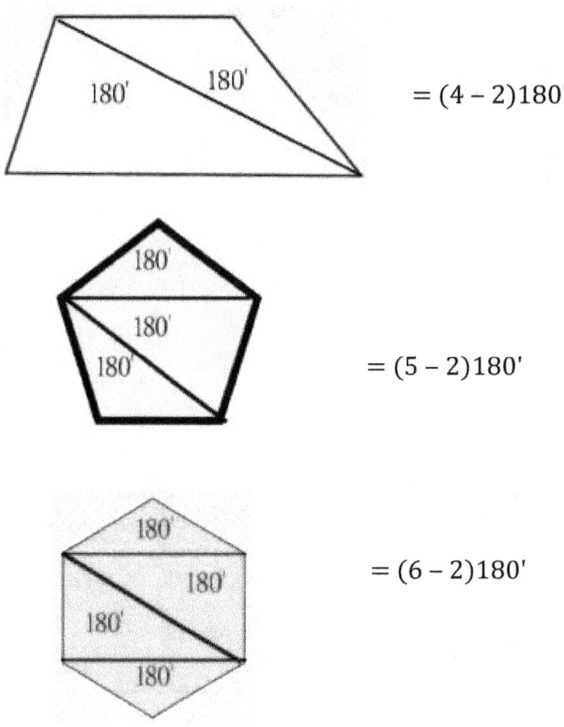

$= (4 - 2)180'$

$= (5 - 2)180'$

$= (6 - 2)180'$

For a *'n' side figure sum of interior angles* $= (n - 2)180'$

2. Sum of Exterior Angles

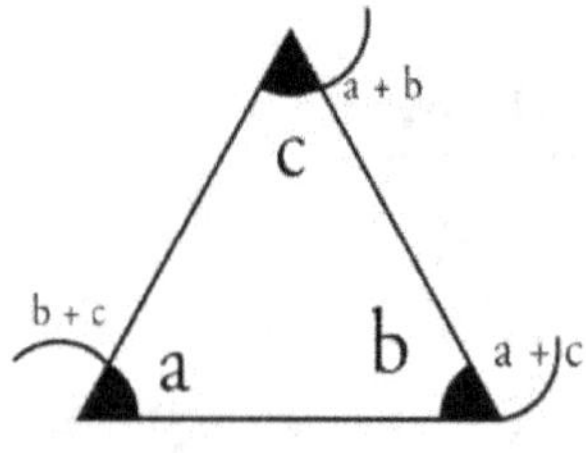

Triangle = a + b + b + c + a + c

Triangle = 2 (a + b + c) = 2(180') = 360'

Sum of exterior angles in a Quadrilateral = $4 \times 90' = 360'$

Similarly for a 'n' $sided\ figure\ sum\ of\ exterior\ angles\ = 360'$

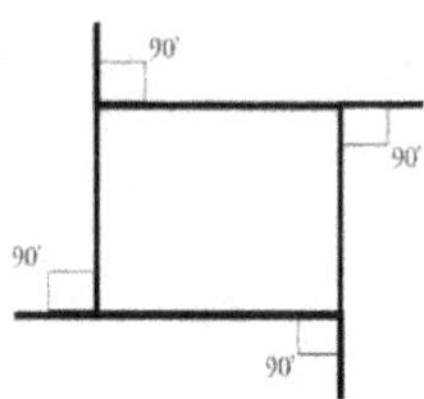

Sum of exterior angles in a polygon is always 360'.

3)Number of Diagonals

No of diagonal in a polygon = $\frac{n(n-3)}{2}$

Where n = no of sides in the polygon.

4)Regular Polygon

If all the sides and angles in a polygon are equal than we call as a regular Polygon.

Circles

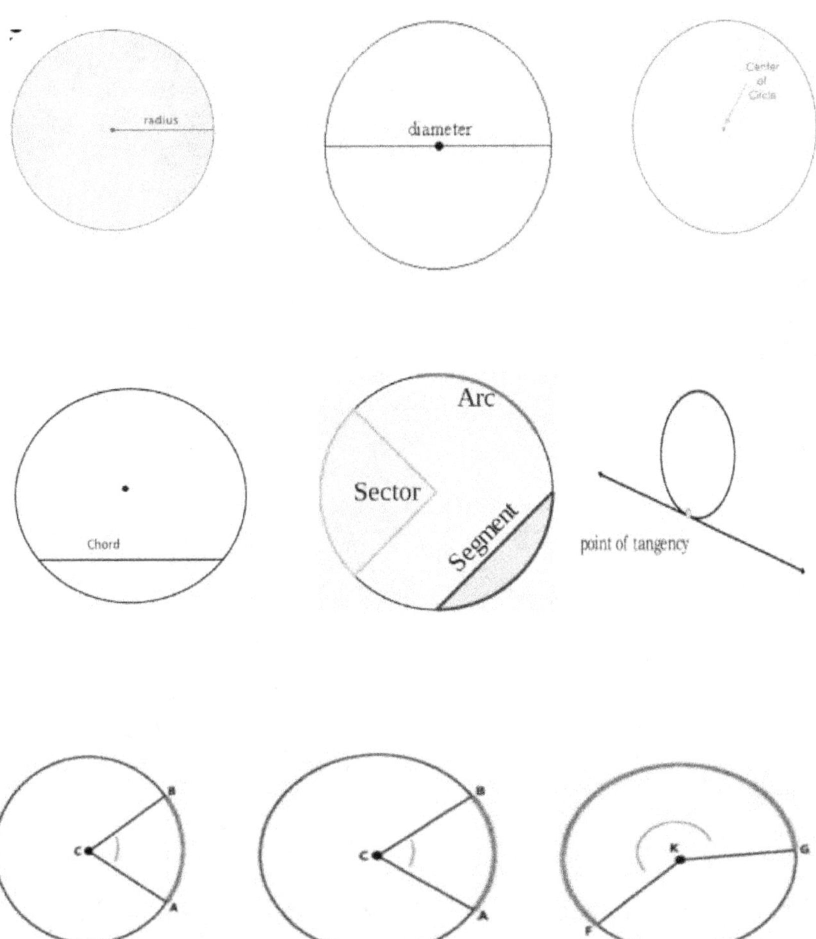
radius
diameter
Center of Circle
Chord
Arc
Sector
Segment
point of tangency
B
C
A
Minor Arc
B
C
A
Minor Arc
K
G
F
Major Arc

Circle

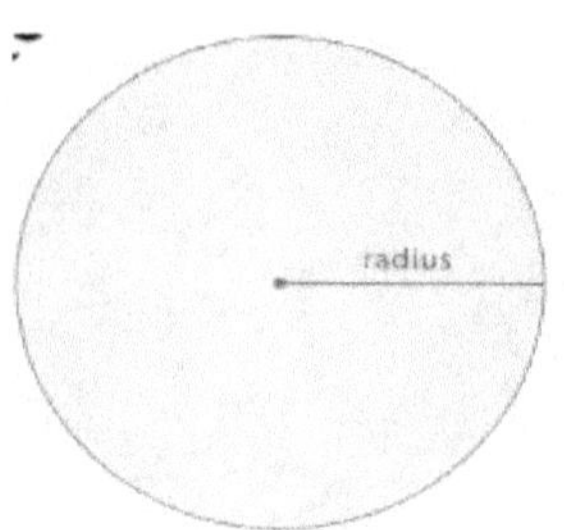

Area of a Circle = πr^2

Circumference of Circle = $2\pi r$

Arc

Whatever it happens at center the same will be reflected on the circle

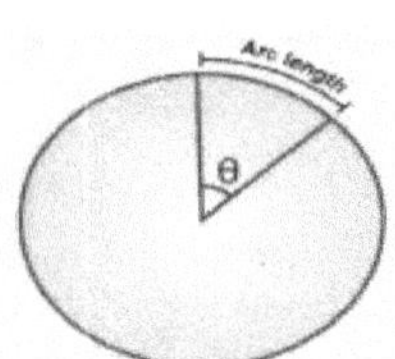

$$\frac{\theta}{360^{\theta}} = \frac{length\ of\ Arc}{Circumference\ of\ circle}$$

$$\frac{\theta}{360^{\theta}} = \frac{L}{2\pi r}$$

$$Length\ of\ Arc = 2\pi r\left(\frac{\theta}{360}\right)$$

Sector

Whatever it happens at center the same will be reflected on the circle

$$\frac{\theta}{360^{\theta}} = \frac{Area\ of\ sector}{\pi r^2}$$

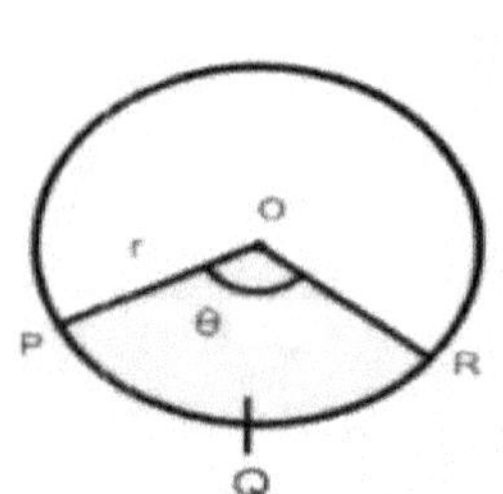

$$\frac{\theta}{360^{\theta}} = \frac{1}{2\pi r}$$

$$Arc\ of\ Sector = \left(\frac{\theta}{360}\right) \times \pi r$$

$Perimeter\ of\ Sector = Length\ of\ Arc + 2radius$

$$Perimeter\ of\ circle = \frac{\theta}{360} \times 2\pi r + 2r$$

$$Perimeter\ of\ circle = (\theta + 2)$$

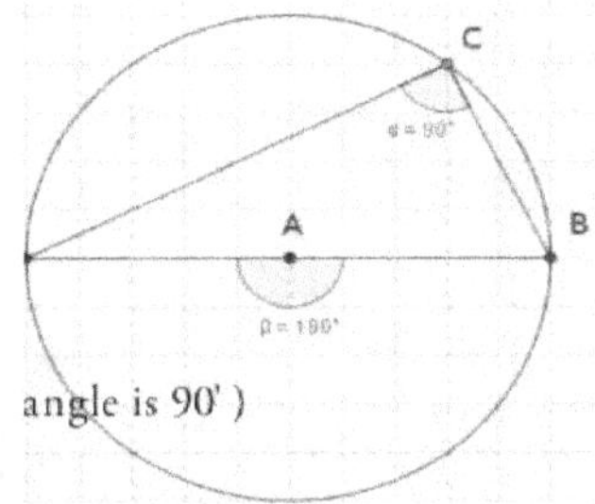

Semicircle

$Angle\ of\ Semi - circle = 180^{\theta}$

$Angle\ of\ Semi - circle = 90^{\theta}$

(Any triangle you draw in a semicircle its angle is 90)

Reason for Angle in a Semi-Circle is 90'

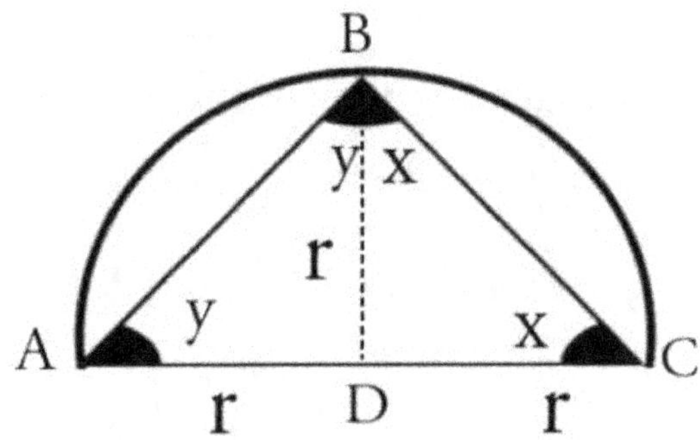

If two sides are equal than there opposite angles are equal

So AD=DB , DC=DB So opposite angle to that sides also equal

Sum of angle in a triangle is 180'

$y + y + x + x = 180'$

$2(x + y) = 180'$

$x + y = 90$

So, Angle in a Semi-Circle is 90'

Important Result in Circles:

Angles in the same segment are equal

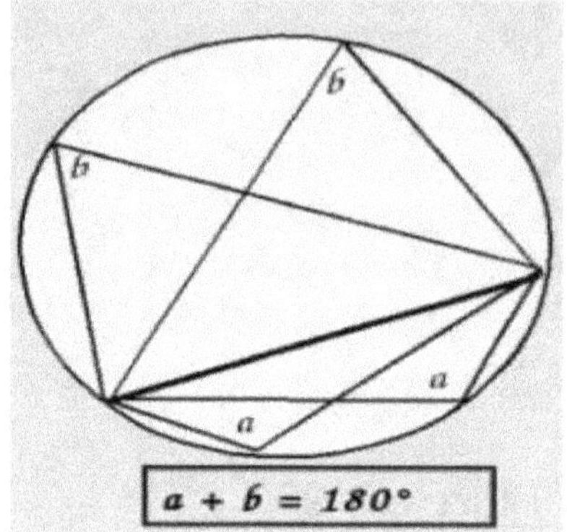

All angles drawn from a chord will have the same angle where they touch the circle. Also the two angles of opposite sides of the chord add up to 180^0

Angle at center is double the angle at circle.

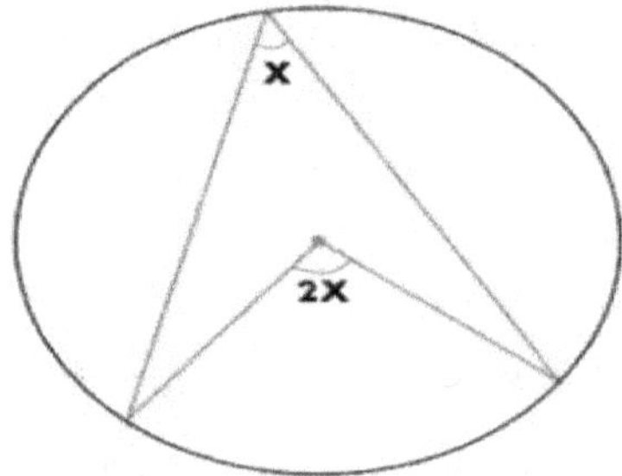

Center to tangent of a circle the angle is always 90:

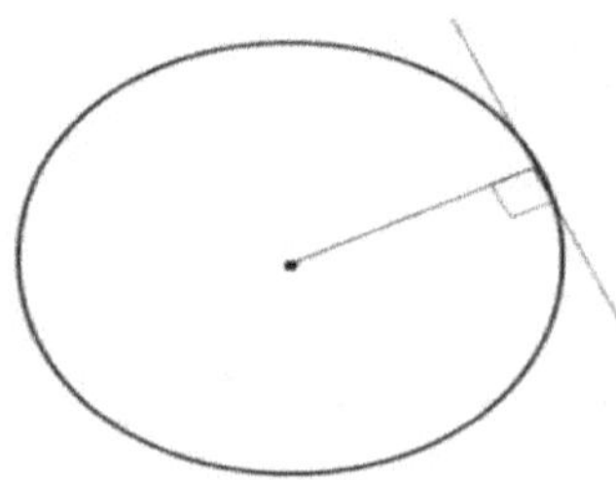

Line joining the mid-point of Chord to Center is always 90°.

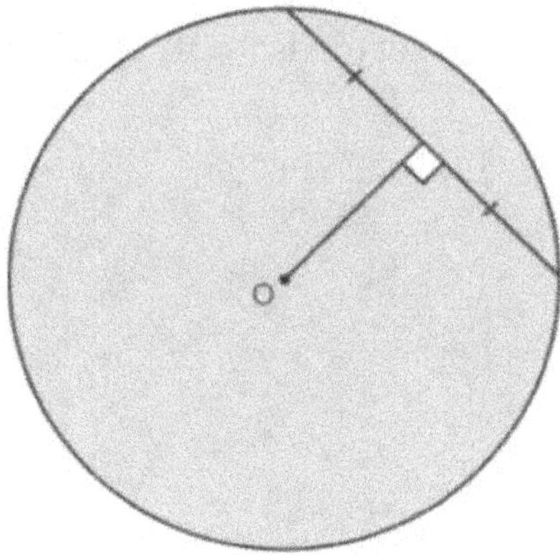

A Quadrilateral fixed inside a circle is Cyclic Quadrilateral In any Cyclic Quadrilateral Sum of opposite Angles are 180°

Here $x+y = p+q = 180°$

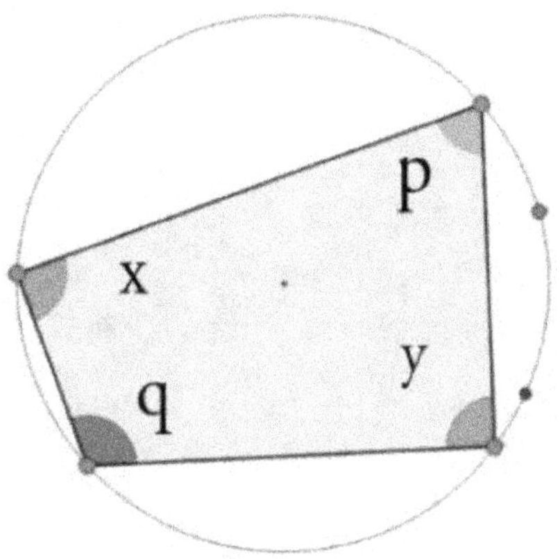

Circle is inscribed in a Quadrilateral

Here AB + DC = AD + BC

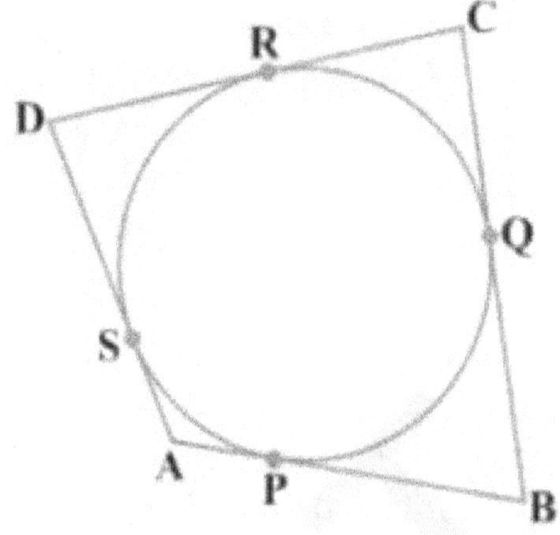

3-D Geometry

Name	Shape	Lateral Surface Area	Total Surface Area	Volum e	Length of Longest Rod
Cuboid		$2lb + 2bh$	$2lb + 2bh + 2h$	lbh	$\sqrt{l^2 + b^2 + h^2}$
Cube		$2a^2 + 2a^2 =$	$2a^2 + 2a^2 + 2a$	$a \, x \, a \, x \, a =$	$\sqrt{3}$
Cylinde r		$2\pi rh$	$2\pi rh + 2\pi r^2$	$\pi r^2 h$	$\sqrt{4r^2 + h^2}$
Cone		πrl	$\pi rl + \pi r^2$	$\frac{1}{3} r^2 h$	" l " (Straight Height)
Sphere		----	$4\pi r^2$	$\frac{1}{4}\pi r^3$	$2r$
Hemi-Sphere		$2\pi r^2$	$2\pi r^2 + \pi r^3 = 3$	$\frac{2}{3}\pi r^3$	$2r$
Prism		Perimeter of Base x Height	Perimeter of Base x Height + top area + bottom area	Area of Base x Height	----
Pyrami d		Perimeter of Base x slant Height	L.S.A + Area of Base	$\frac{1}{3} \times Area$ Base x Height	Slant Height

Co-ordinate Geometry

Co-ordinate Plain

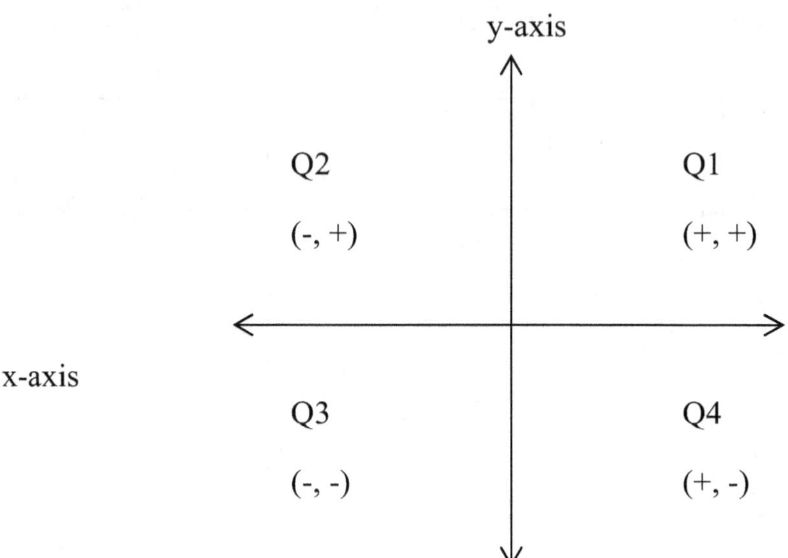

Distance and Slope

$A(x_1,y_1)$

$B(x_2,y_2)$

1. Distance $AB = \sqrt{(x_2 - x_1)^2 + (y_2 - y_1)^2}$

2. Slope $m = \frac{Rise}{Run} = \frac{y_2 - y_1}{x_2 - x_1}$

$$Slope = tan\theta = \frac{Opp\ side}{Adj\ Side} = \frac{y_2 - y_1}{x_2 - x_1} = \frac{Rise}{Run}$$

Dividing a line

3. $$Mid\ point\ \text{C} = \left(\frac{x_1 + x_2}{2}, \frac{y_1 + y_2}{2}\right)$$

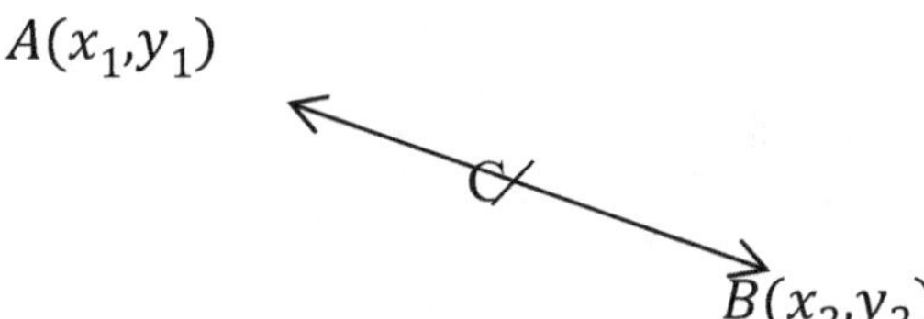

4. $$C = \left(\frac{mx_2 + nx_1}{2}, \frac{my_2 + ny_1}{2}\right)$$

$A(x_1, y_1)$ m n

$B(x_2, y_2)$

5. If two lines are perpendicular then

$$Product\ of\ slopes = m_1 \times m_2 = -1$$

$$Prependicular\ line\ slope = -\frac{1}{m}$$

m1

m2

6. **Intercepts of a Line**

$$ax + by + c = 0$$

X-intercept (Replace 'y' with '0')

$ax + b(0) + c = 0$

$ax =- c$

$x =- \frac{c}{a}$

Y-intercept (Replace 'x' with '0')

$a(0) + by + c = 0$

$by =- c$

$y =- \frac{c}{b}$

7. **Line equations**

Given values	Lines Equation
$Slope\ "m"$	$y = mx$
$Slope\ "m",\ y - intercept = c$	$y = mx + c$
$Slope\ "m", point(x_1,y_1)$	$y - y_1 = m(x - x_1)$
$point(x_1,y_1), point(x_2,y_2)$	

$$\frac{y - y_1}{y_1 - y_2} = \frac{x - x1}{x_1 - x_2}$$

$x - intercept = a, y - intercept = b$ $\quad \frac{x}{a} + \frac{y}{b} = 1$

8. Equation of line parallel to $x - axis$

$$y = a$$

Equation of line parallel to $y - axis$

$$y = b$$

ALGEBRA

Algebra

1. Algebraic Expression

It contains operations, variables and constants.

Example:-

$$3x + 4y + 3$$

Here

$x, y \rightarrow variables$

$3 \quad \rightarrow constant$

$+ , - \rightarrow operation$

2. Algebraic Equation

If an algebraic expression is equated to a value then it is an algebraic equation.

Example:-

$3x^2 + 2y + 3 = 0$

$3x^2 = Monomial$

$3x^2 + 2y = Binomial$

$3x^2 + 2y + 3 = trinomial$

3. Roots of an Equation

$$x^2 + x - 6 = 0$$

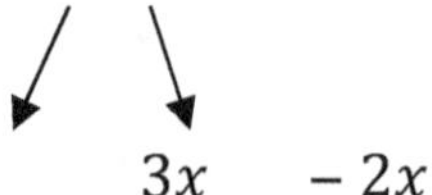

$3x \quad - 2x$

$x^2 + 3x - 2x - 6 = 0$

$x(x + 3) - 2(x + 3) = 0$

$(x - 2)(x + 3) = 0$

$x - 2 = 0 \quad (or) \quad x + 3 = 0$

$x = 2 \quad (or) \quad x = -3$

Roots of an equation $for\ ax^2 + bx + c = 0$.

If α,β are the roots of an equation.

$$\alpha, \beta = \frac{-b \pm \sqrt{b^2 - 4ac}}{2a}$$

$$\alpha = \frac{-b + \sqrt{b^2 - 4ac}}{2a}$$

$$\beta = \frac{-b - \sqrt{b^2 - 4ac}}{2a}$$

$if\ b^2 - 4ac = 0\ (Roots\ are\ real\ and\ equal)$

$if\ b^2 - 4ac > 0\ (Roots\ are\ real\ and\ Distinct)$

$if\ b^2 - 4ac < 0\ (Roots\ are\ Imaginary)$

If α, β are the roots of an Equation $ax^2 + bx + c = 0$

$$\alpha + \beta = -\frac{b}{a} (Sum\ of\ the\ Roots)$$

$$\alpha\beta = \frac{c}{a}$$ (Product of the Roots)

Example:-

Find the roots of the equation, type of roots, sum of roots and product of roots for the given equation $x^2 + x - 6 = 0$?

Solution:

Here a = 1, b = 1 and c = -6

(a)

$$\alpha = \frac{-b + \sqrt{b^2 - 4ac}}{2a}$$

$$\alpha = \frac{-1 + \sqrt{1^2 - 4(1)(-6)}}{2(1)}$$

$$\alpha = \frac{-1 + \sqrt{1 + 24}}{2}$$

$$\alpha = \frac{-1 + \sqrt{25}}{2}$$

$$\alpha = \frac{-1 + 5}{2}$$

$$\alpha = \frac{4}{2}$$

$$\alpha = 2$$

$$\beta = \frac{-b-\sqrt{b^2-4ac}}{2a}$$

$$\beta = \frac{-1-\sqrt{1^2-4(1)(-6)}}{2(1)}$$

$$\beta = \frac{-1-\sqrt{1+24}}{2}$$

$$\beta = \frac{-1-\sqrt{25}}{2}$$

$$\beta = \frac{-1-5}{2}$$

$$\beta = \frac{-6}{2}$$

$$\beta = -3$$

(b)

$$b^2-4ac = (1)^2-4(1)(-6)$$

$$= 1+24$$

$$= 25$$

$Here\ b^2-4ac > 0 \quad then\ roots\ are\ real\ and\ distint$

(c)

$$\alpha+\beta = -\frac{b}{a} = -\frac{1}{1} = -1$$

$$\alpha\beta = \frac{c}{a} = \frac{-6}{1} = -6$$

4. Exponents

1. $a^m \times a^n = a^{m+n}$
2. $\frac{a^m}{a^n} = a^{m-n}$
3. $(a^m)^n = a^{mn}$
4. $a^{-n} = \frac{1}{a^n}$
5. $a^m \times b^m = (ab)^m$
6. $a^0 = 1\ (where\ a \neq 0)$
7. $\sqrt[n]{a} = a^{\frac{1}{n}}$

5. Basic Formulas

1. $(x+y)^2 = x^2 + 2xy + y^2$
2. $(x-y)^2 = x^2 - 2xy + y^2$
3. $(x+y)(x-y) = x^2 - y^2$
4. $(x+y)^3 = x^3 + 3x^2y + 3xy^2 + y^3$
5. $(x-y)^3 = x^3 - 3x^2y + 3xy^2 - y^3$
6. $(x+y+z)^2 = x^2 + y^2 + z^2 + 2xy + 2yz + 2zx$
7. $x^3 + y^3 = (x+y)(x^2 - xy + y^2)$
8. $x^3 - y^3 = (x+y)(x^2 + xy + y^2)$

6. Functions

An algebraic expression in one variable is known as a function.

Example: $f(x) = x^3 - 3x^2 + 9$

a) Special Function:-

An algebraic expression defining the definition of an operation is called special function.

Example: $If\ a \# b = a^3 - ab^2 + 2\ then\ find\ 3 \# 2$?

Solution:

$3 \# 2 = (3)^3 - (3)(2)^2 + 2$

$3 \# 2 = 27 - 12 + 2$

$3 \# 2 = 17$

7. Simple Equations

Example 1: Solve the equations

$$2x + 4y = 16$$

$$3x - 2y = 0$$

$Try\ to\ make\ coefficient\ of\ either\ x\ or\ y\ as\ equal$

So multiply Equation 2 with ‘2’ to make both the ‘y’ coefficients equal.

$$2x + 4y = 16$$

$$2(3x - 2y) = 0$$

$$\begin{array}{r} 2x + 4y = 16 \\ 6x - 4y = 0 \\ \hline 8x = 16 \end{array}$$

$$x = \frac{16}{8} = 2$$

$replace\ "x"\ value\ in\ equation\ 1$

$2(2) + 4y = 16$

$4 + 4y = 16$

4y=16-4

4y=12

$$y = \frac{12}{4} = 3$$

Example 2:

Solve

$$2x + 4y = 10$$

$$8x + 16y = 40$$

Solution: Here Multiply Equation 1 with '4' to make both the 'x' coefficients equal

$Eq - \boxed{1} => \quad 4(2x + 4y = 10)$

$$8x + 16y = 40$$

$$8x + 16y = 40$$

Here after multiplying with '4' both the equations appear as one and the same. Here two same lines intersect at infinite many points so we have infinite solutions.

Example 3:

Solve

$$2x + 4y = 10$$

$$8x + 16y = 90$$

Solution: Here Multiply Equation 1 with '4' to make both the 'x' coefficients equal

$Eq - \boxed{1} \quad 4(2x + 4y = 10)$

$Eq - \boxed{2} \quad 8x + 16y = 90$

$$8x + 16y = 40$$

$$8x + 16y = 90$$

Here both are same equations but constant is different it means both the lines represent set of parallel lines. As parallel lines will not intersect there will be zero solutions.

Example 4 (Solving 2 equations with 3 unknowns)

1. *Find the values of x and y*

$$x + 2y + 3z = 10$$

$$3x + 4y + 9z = 26$$

Solution:

Here we have 2 equations and 3 unknowns (x,y,z). Generally to find 3 unknowns we need 3 equations, but in some special cases we can find values of some variables.

$Eq - (1) \rightarrow 3(x + 2y + 3z = 10) \rightarrow 3x + 6y + 9z = 30$

$$3x + 4y + 9z = 26$$

$$- \quad - \quad - \quad -$$

$$2y = 4$$

$$y = 2$$

Here 'x' and 'z' are parallel lines so we can find 'y' value in this case but we can't find 'x' or 'z' values.

<u>**Note**</u>: - Even with 3 unknowns and 2 equations, sometimes we can find a value.

8. Inequalities and absolute values

In inequalities we come across > (greater), < (lesser), ≥ (greater or equal), ≤ (lesser or equal).

Example:-

$3x + 4 \geq 2x + 7$

$3x - 2x \geq 7 - 4$

$x \geq 3$

$x \leq 3$

$3x + 4 \leq 2x + 7$

$3x - 2x \leq 7 - 4$

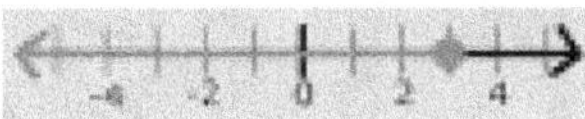

$3x + 4 > 2x + 7$

$3x - 2x > 7 - 4$

$x > 3$

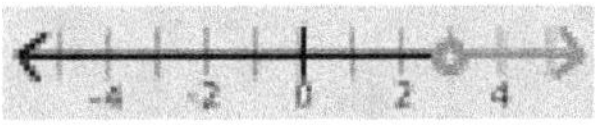

$3x + 4 < 2x + 7$

$3x - 2x < 7 - 4$

$x < 3$

a) <u>Arithmetic operation on inequalities:</u>

Let us apply all the arithmetic operations on 8 > 6

Addition →		8 + 2 > 6 + 2	(Correct)
Subtraction →		8 - 2 > 6 – 2	(Correct)
+ive	Multiplication →	8 x 2 > 6 x 2	(Correct)
+ive	Division →	8/2 > 6/2	(Correct)
-ive	Multiplication →	8 x - 2 > 6 x - 2	(Incorrect)

-ive Division → 8/-2 > 6/-2 (Incorrect)

Note:

When we multiply or divide an inequality with a negative number the inequality flips.

Example:-

$$-3x > 9$$

Dividing both sides with "− 3"

$$\frac{-3x}{-3} < \frac{9}{-3}$$

$$x < -3$$

Example:-

$$x^2 > y^2$$

We can't say $x > y$

because x,y may also be negative values. So we can't find the relation between x and y

b) <u>Absolute Values(| |):</u>

<u>Case 1:</u>

If $|x| = 5$ => $x = +5$ (or) $x = -5$

<u>Case 2:</u>

$|x| \geq 5$ => $x \leq -5$ (or) $x \geq +5$

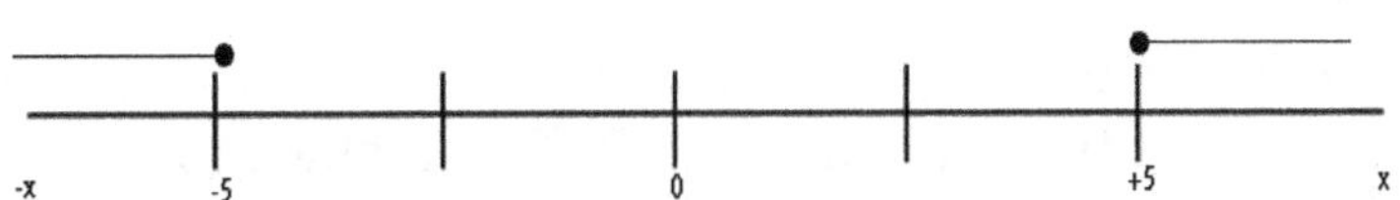

<u>Case 3:</u>

$|x| \leq 5$ => $-5 \leq x \leq 5$

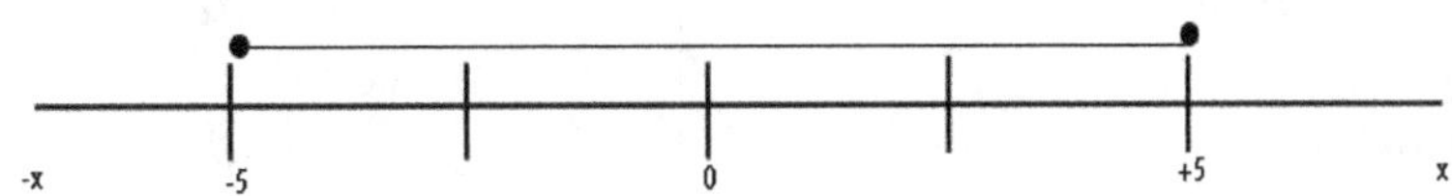

Case 4:

$if\ |x| - 3 < 0$

$|x| < 3$

$-3 < x < 3$

$|x| - 3 > 0$

$|x| > 3$

$x < -3\ \&\ x > +3$

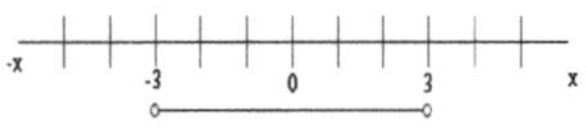

C) Solving a Quadratic Inequality:

1. $Find\ the\ roots\ of\ Equation\ x^2 - 4x + 3 = 0$

$x^2 - 3x - x + 3 = 0$

$x(x-3) - 1(x-3) = 0$

$(x-3)(x-1) = 0$

$(x-3) = 0 \quad or \quad (x-1) = 0$

$x = 3 \quad or \quad x = 1$

2. Find the roots of In equation equation

$x^2 - 4x + 3 \geq 0$

$(x-3)(x-1) \geq 0$

$+\ and\ +$

(Or)

$-\ and\ -$

Case 1: $+\ and\ +$

3. Find the roots of In

$x^2 - 4x + 3 \leq 0$

$(x-3)(x-1) \leq 0$

$-\ and\ +$

(Or)

$+\ and\ -$

Case 1: $-\ and\ +$

$(x-3) \geq 0 \quad \& \quad (x-1) \geq 0$

$x \geq 3 \quad \& \quad x \geq 1$

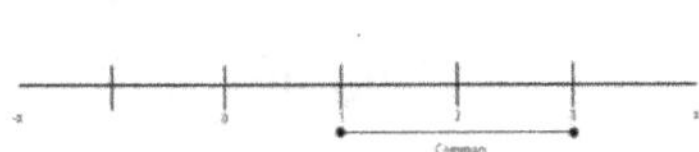

Here common intersection is $x \geq 3$

Case 2: $-$ *and* $-$

$x - 3 \leq 0 \quad \& \quad x - 1 \leq 0$

$x \leq 3 \quad \& \quad x \leq 1$

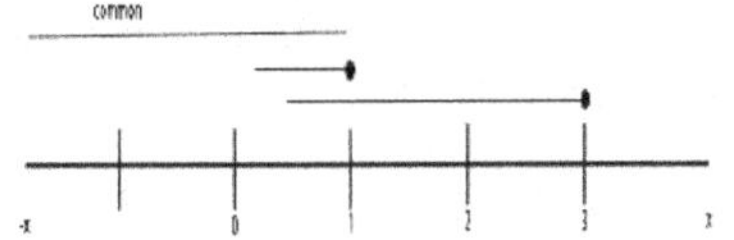

Here common intersection is $x \leq 1$ *On combining both case 1 and case 2*

$x \in (-\alpha, 1] \cup [3, \alpha)$

$(x-3) \leq 0 \; \& \; (x-1) \geq 0$

$x \leq 3 \quad \& \quad x \geq 1$

Here common intersection is $1 \leq x \leq 3$

Case 2: $+$ *and* $-$

$x - 3 \geq 0 \quad \& \quad x - 1 \leq 0$

$x \geq 3 \quad \& \quad x \leq 1$

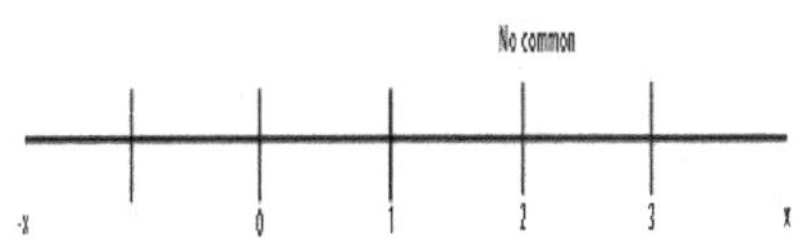

Here no common intersection On combining both case1 and case 2

$x \in [1, 3]$

4. Find the roots of In equation	5. Find the roots of In equation
$x^2 - 4x + 3 > 0$	$x^2 - 4x + 3 > 0$
Here equality is taken out so 1,3 is not included in the solution set	Here equality is taken is out not so 1,3 is not included in the solution set
$x^2 - 4x + 3 < 0$ $x \in (-\alpha, 1) \cup (3, \alpha)$	$x \in (1, 3)$

d) Different solutions possible for a Quadratic Expression

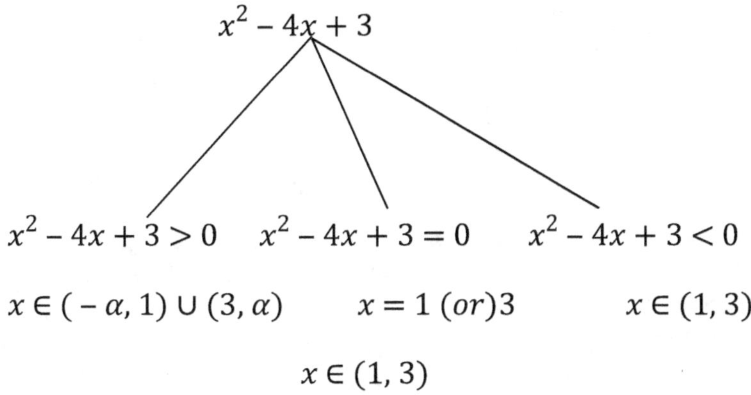

e) Graphical Representation:

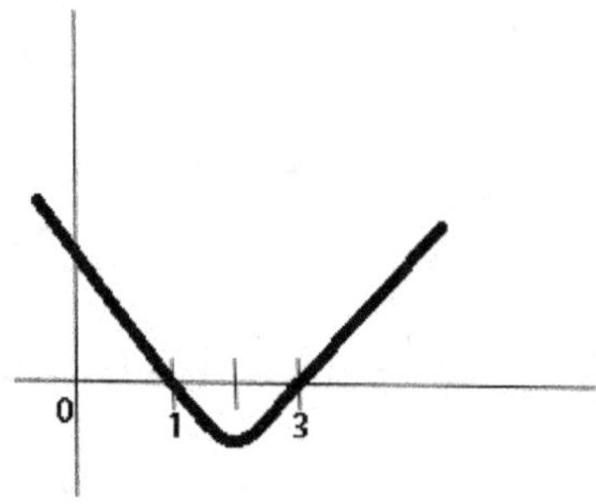

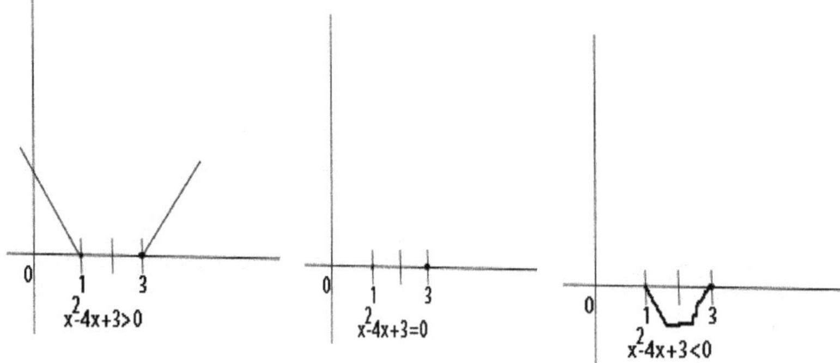

f) Range of Roots for inequations:-

$if\ p,q\ are\ the\ roots\ of\ an\ Inequation\ ax^2 + bx + c = 0\ then$

$ax^2 + bx + c \geq 0$ & $ax^2 + bx + c \leq 0$

$x \in (-\alpha, p] \cup [q, \alpha)$ $x \in [P, q]$

$ax^2 + bx + c > 0$ $ax^2 + bx + c < 0$

$x \in (-\alpha, p) \cup (q, \alpha)$ $x \in (p, q)$

COUNTING

Permutations and Combinations

a) Difference between permutation and combination

What is the difference between Permutation and Combination?

Permutation (Arrangement)	Combination (Selection)
Example:	Example:
How to arrange A, B, C by taking 2 at a time	How to select A, B, C by taking 2 at a time
AB BC CA BA CB AC	AB BC CA
(Here order matter)	(Here Order doesn't matter) AB ←→ BA Selecting AB is same as selecting BA
No of ways = 6	No of ways = 3
Example : In how many ways 3 many different prizes can be given to persons who secured 1st, 2nd and 3rd prize in a running race	Example :In how ways we can pick 3 players for a football team?

Solution: Let X, Y and Z are 3 persons

1st	2nd	3rd	1st	2nd	3rd
X	Y	Z	Z	Y	X

Solution: Here 3rd prize winner and 1st prize Winner can't exchange their places, because the 1st prize is different from 3rd prize

(Here order is important so it is a Permutation question)

Here order doesn't matter, because in whatever the order we select all three Persons will be in the team (So it is a Combinations question)

In how many way 3 people can be be arrange from a group of 10 people

How many people required required

3

So draw 3 slots

___ ___ ___

Fill possibilities in slots and multiply

$$\frac{10}{\delta} \times \frac{9}{\delta} \times \frac{8}{\delta} = 720\ ways$$

It is like

In how many ways 3 people can selected from a group of 10 people.

How many people

3

So draw 3 slots

___ ___ ___

Fill possibilities and divide the slots by slot no

$$\frac{10}{1} \times \frac{9}{2} \times \frac{8}{3} = 120 ways$$

$$n_{P_r} = \frac{n!}{(n-r)!}$$

$$10_{P_3} = \frac{10!}{7!}$$

$$= \frac{10 \times 9 \times 8 \times 7!}{7!} = 720\ ways$$

$$n_{C_r} = \frac{n!}{(n-r)!r!}$$

$$10_{C_3} = \frac{10!}{7!3!}$$

$$= \frac{10 \times 9 \times 8 \times 7!}{7! \times 3 \times 2 \times 1} = 120 \text{ ways}$$

(The same formula application I explained in a simpler way)

b) Basic Approach for Permutations and Combinations

Step 1:- Identify what is your target (what you are supposed to find)

Step 2:- Draw appropriate slots and fill the numbers.

Step 3:- Check whether order matters or order doesn't matter.

Step 4:- If order matters don't divide with the slot number and if order doesn't matter divide with slot number.

Example 1: In a class there are 30 students, if each student gives a handshake to every other student, then find the total number of handshakes possible?

Solution:-

Step 1:- My target is to find number of handshakes, in order to form a Hand shake I need two persons.
Step 2:- Even I interchange 2 persons there is no change in the Hand shake formed, so order doesn't matter.

Step 3:- _________ _________ (draw slots)

30 x 29 (fill the feasible number)

Step 4:-

$$\frac{30}{1} \times \frac{29}{2} = 435$$

$(Here\ order\ doesn't\ matter\ so\ divide\ by\ slot\ number)$

c) Conditional slots

Example 2: Find the total number of diagonals in an octagon?

Solution:-

Step 1:- Target is to find total number of diagonals

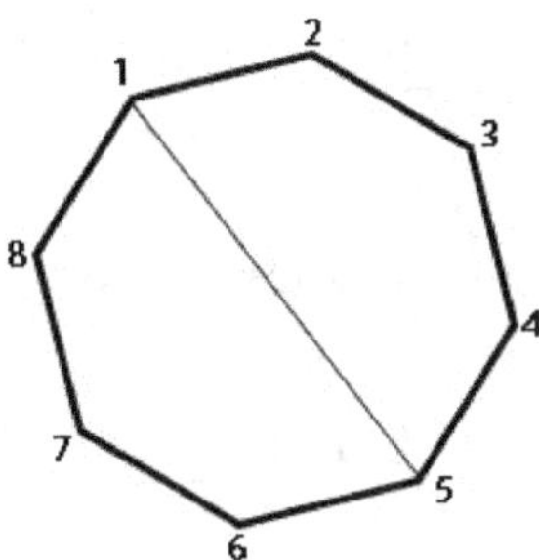

Step 2:- If I select '1' as first vertex and 5 as second vertex (or) '5' as a first vertex and '1' as second vertex I get same diagonal, so order doesn't matter.

Step 3:- ________ ________ (Draw slots as per requirement)

8 5

You can select any vertices — Conditional slot you can't select the two adjacent slots

Step 4:-

$$\frac{8}{1} \times \frac{5}{2} = \frac{40}{2} = 20\ diagonals$$

(Order doesn't matter so divide by slot number)

Multiple Slots

Example 3: In how many ways we can pick 3 boys and 2 girls from a group of 5 boys and 6 girls.

Solution: Here multiple slots model comes into picture

Step 1: Boys = 5 Girls = 6

Pick Boys = 3 Girls = 2

Step 2:- Here 'Select' word was directly given in the question so it is a selection problem.

Step 3:- Boys * Girls (Draw slots as per requirement)

Step 4: Here boys can be selected only from group of boys and girls can be selected only from group of girls

$$\frac{5}{1} \times \frac{4}{2} \times \frac{3}{3} \times \frac{6}{1} \times \frac{5}{2} = 150\ \text{ways}$$

Boys Girls

Example 4: Find total number of squares and rectangles in the figure given below?

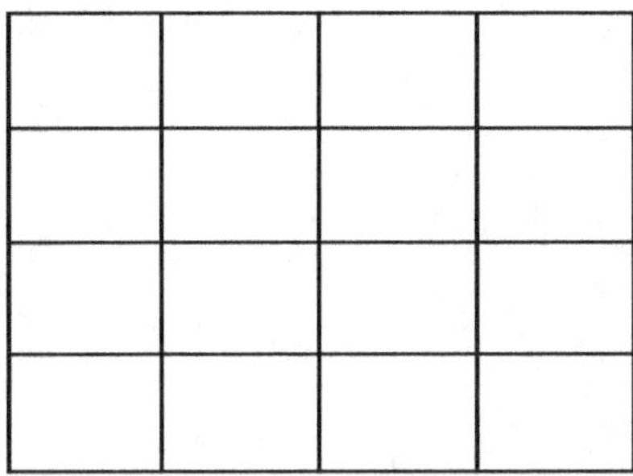

Solution:

Step 1:- Here I require 2 horizontal and 2 vertical lines to form my target which is either a Square/ Rectangle.

Step 2:- Order doesn't matter because selection of lines order doesn't matter

Step 3: Draw two slots one for horizontal and one for vertical here total Horizontal lines =5 and Vertical lines =5, we need to

select Horizontal =2 and Vertical =2.

Step 3:- $\dfrac{\frac{5}{1}\times\frac{4}{2}}{Horizontal}\times\dfrac{\frac{5}{1}\times\frac{4}{2}}{Vertical}=100$

Probability

a) Basic Formulas

(1) $$P(E) = \frac{Chance\ to\ occur\ event\ 'E'}{Total\ No\ of\ \ Possible\ Outcomes}$$

(2) Since Denominator $\geq$ Numerator, $0 \leq P(E) \leq 1$

P (E) =0 (Event never happens)

P (E)=0.5 (Event is equally likely to occur or not to occur)

P (E)=1 (Event will happen for sure)

(3) $P(\bar{E}) = 1 - P(E)$ or $P(E)+P(\bar{E})=1$

Example 1: If a coin is tossed what is the probability of getting

a) Neither Head nor tail

b) A Head

c) Either Head or tail

a) Neither Head nor tail

P(E)=0 (Because if we toss a coin either head or a tail will definitely be the outcome)

b) Getting a Head

Total possibilities = {H, T}

P(H) = ½

c) Either Head or tail

P(E) =1 (Because if we toss a coin either head or a tail will definitely be the outcome)

Example 2: Probability of rain on Day 1 is 2/5, Day 2 is 3/5 and Day 3 is 5/6. What is the probability of rain at least on one day?

Sol:- At least one day means

$$P(D_1\bar{D}_2\bar{D}_3) + P(\bar{D}_1 D_2\bar{D}_3) + P(\bar{D}_1\bar{D}_2 D_3) + P(D_1 D_2\bar{D}_3)$$

$$+ P(\bar{D}_1 D_2 D_3) + P(D_1\bar{D}_2 D_3) + P(D_1 D_2 D_3)$$

(OR)

P(Rain on at least one day) = 1-P(No rain on 3 Days)

$$= 1 - (\bar{D}_1\bar{D}_2\bar{D}_3)$$

Here

$$P(D_1) = \frac{2}{5} \qquad P(D_2) = \frac{3}{5} \qquad P(D_3) = \frac{5}{6}$$

$$P(\bar{D}_1) = \frac{3}{5} \qquad P(\bar{D}_2) = \frac{2}{5} \qquad P(\bar{D}_3) = \frac{1}{6}$$

$$= 1 - P(\bar{D}_1) \ X \ P(\bar{D}_2) \ X \ P(\bar{D}_3)$$

$$= 1 - \frac{3}{5} X \frac{2}{5} X \frac{1}{6}$$

$$= 1 - \frac{1}{25}$$

$$= \frac{24}{25}$$

b) <u>Independent Event</u>

If the outcome of first event does not affect the outcome of second
event then two events are said to be independent.

P (A and B) = P (A) x P (B)

P (A or B) = P (A) + P (B)

Example:

A bag contains 4 red balls, 6 blue balls and 8 green balls. When 2 balls are drawn, what is the probability of getting

(i) One red and one blue with replacement
(ii) One red or one blue with replacement
(iii)

Red=4 blue=6 Green=8 total=18

P (red and blue) = P (red) x P (blue)

$$\frac{4}{18} \times \frac{6}{18} = \frac{2}{27}$$

P (red or blue) = P (red) + P (blue)

$$\frac{4}{18} + \frac{6}{18} = \frac{5}{9}$$

c) Dependent Event

The outcome of first event affects the outcome of second event then two events are said to be dependent.

P (A and B) = P (A) x P (B after A's affect)

P (A or B) = P (A) + P (B) – P (A∩B)

Examples

Example 1: A bag contains 4 red balls,6 blue balls and 8 green balls. What is the probability of getting 2 red balls without replacement?

Red=4 blue=6 Green=8 total=18

P (red and red) = P (red) x P (red)

$$\frac{4}{18} \times \frac{3}{17} = \frac{2}{51}$$

(Here the possibility of getting second red ball is affected by the result of first red ball.)

Example 2: When a card is drawn from a deck of cards what is the probability of getting a king or a heart card?

King cards=4 Hearts=13 King of Heart=1 total=52

P (King of Heart) = P (King) + P (Heart) –P (King of Heart)

$$\frac{4}{52} + \frac{13}{52} - \frac{1}{52} = \frac{4}{13}$$

d)Types of Questions

(i)Coins

(ii)Dice

(iii)Cards

(i) Coins

Coin(1)= {H, T} $\mathbf{2^1}$

Coin(2) = {(H,T) (T,H) (H,H) (T,T)} **2^2**

Coin(3) = {(H,H,H) (T,T,T) (H,T,T) (
T,H,T) (T,T,H) (T,H,H) (H,T,H) (H,H,T)} **2^3**

Coin (n) = {……………….} **2^n**

(ii) Dice

Die (1) = {1, 2, 3, 4, 5, 6} = 6

Die (2) = {(1, 1) (1, 2) (1, 3) (1, 4) (1, 5) (1, 6)

(2, 1) (2, 2) (2, 3) (2, 4) (2, 5) (2, 6)

(3, 1) (3, 2) (3, 3) (3, 4) (3, 5) (3, 6)

(4, 1) (4, 2) (4, 3) (4, 4) (4, 5) (4, 6)

(5, 1) (5, 2) (5, 3) (5, 4) (5, 5) (5, 6)

(6, 1) (6, 2) (6, 3) (6, 4) (6, 5) (6, 6)}

6^2=36

Die (n) = {……………………………………} **6^n**

When a die is thrown for 2 times the possibility of getting the sum as

2 → 1 (1, 1)

3 →2 (1, 2) (2, 1)

4 →3 (1, 3) (2, 2) (3, 1)

5 →4 (1, 4) (2, 3) (3, 2) (4, 1)

6 →5 (1, 5) (2, 4) (3, 3) (4, 2) (5, 1)

7 →6	(1, 6) (2, 5) (3, 4) (4, 3) (5, 2) (6, 1)
8 →5	(2, 6) (5, 3) (4, 4) (3, 5) (6, 2)
9 →4	(6, 3) (5, 4) (4, 5) (3, 6)
10→3	(6, 4) (5, 5) (4, 6)
11→2	(6, 5) (5, 6)
12→1	(6, 6)

(iv) **Cards**

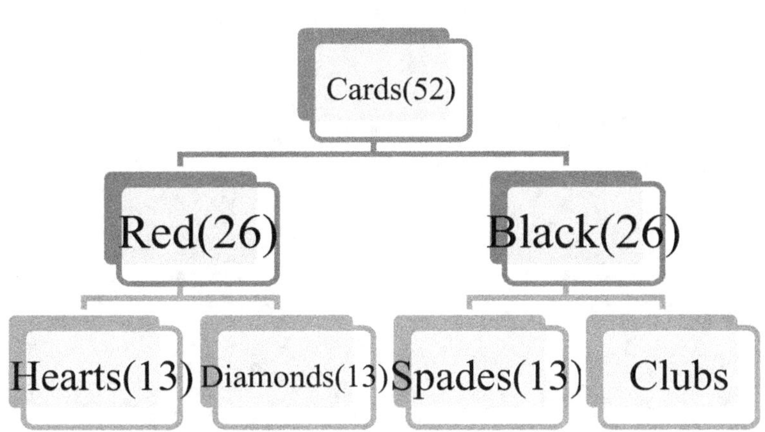

{A, 2, 3, 4, 5, 6, 7, 8, 9, 10, J, Q, K} (4 Sets)

Example : When a coin is tossed 3 times what is the probability of getting

(i) Head on first, Tail on second, Head on third

(ii) 2 Heads and one Tail

Solution:-

(i) Head on first, Tail on second, Head on third

P (H, T, H) = P (H) x P (T) x P (H)

$$= \frac{1}{2} \times \frac{1}{2} \times \frac{1}{2} = \frac{1}{8}$$

(ii) 2 Heads and one Tail

P (H, H, T) or P (H, T, H) or P(T, H, H)

$$= P(H) \times P(H) \times P(T) + P(H) \times P(T) \times P(H) + P(T) \times P(H) \times P(H)$$

$$= \frac{1}{2} \times \frac{1}{2} \times \frac{1}{2} + \frac{1}{2} \times \frac{1}{2} \times \frac{1}{2} + \frac{1}{2} \times \frac{1}{2} \times \frac{1}{2}$$

$$= \frac{1}{8} + \frac{1}{8} + \frac{1}{8} = \frac{3}{8}$$

Sequencing

When you have a question asking the result for a bigger value rather than solving it completely just check for the smaller values and look at the pattern how it was moving.

Examples

Example 1: Find the Average of first 500 odd numbers?

Solution: Tough to find the average of 500 odd numbers in one step. So take small set of data first

Odd numbers

1, 3, 5, 7…………..

$$first\ '2'\ numbers \rightarrow \frac{1+3}{2} = 2$$

$$first\ '3'\ numbers \rightarrow \frac{1+3+5}{3} = 3$$

$$first\ '4'\ numbers \rightarrow \frac{1+3+5+7}{4} = 4$$

Here average of first 2 numbers is 2, first 3 numbers is 3 and first 4 numbers is 4 and so on is the sequence

$$So\ the\ average\ of\ first\ '500'\ Odd\ numbers\ = 500$$

Example 2: Find the total number of squares in a class 8 x 8 chess board?

Solution:

1 x 1 → ☐ → 1 Square

1^2

2 x 2 →

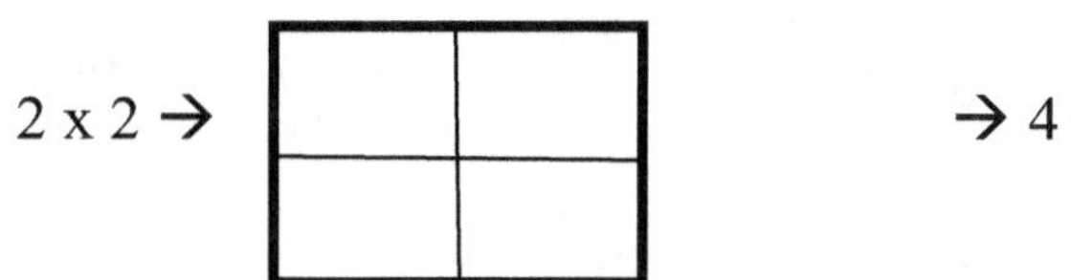

→ 4 + 1

$2^2 + 1^2$

3 x 3 →

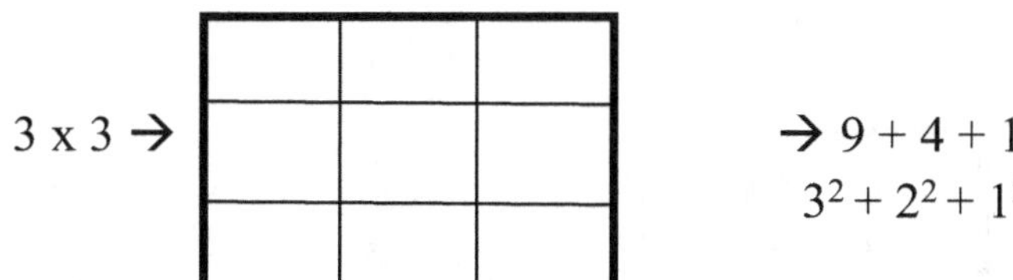

→ 9 + 4 + 1

$3^2 + 2^2 + 1^2$

.

.

.

.

.

8 x 8 →

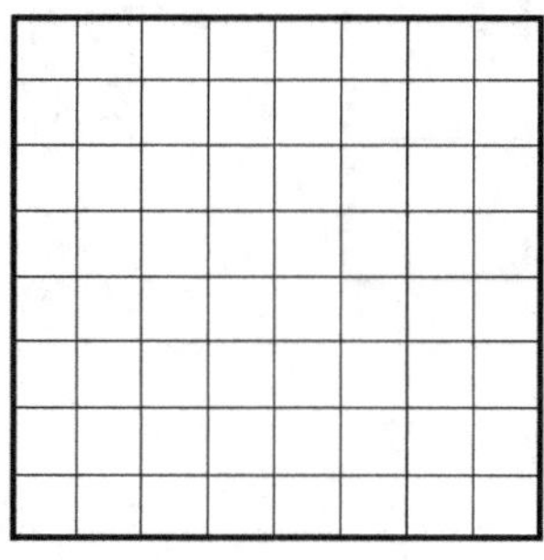

→ $8^2 + 7^2 + \ldots\ldots\ldots\ldots\ldots + 1^2$

Here sequence is $1^2, 2^2 + 1^2, 3^2 + 2^2 + 1^2, \ldots\ldots\ldots\ldots, 8^2 + 7^2 + \ldots\ldots\ldots\ldots\ldots + 1^2$

$$Sum\ of\ square\ of\ first\ 'n'\ natural\ numbers = \frac{n(n+1)(2n+1)}{6}$$

$$= \frac{8(9)(17)}{6}$$

$$= 204\ squares$$

Example 3:Find the total number of rectangles in a class board?

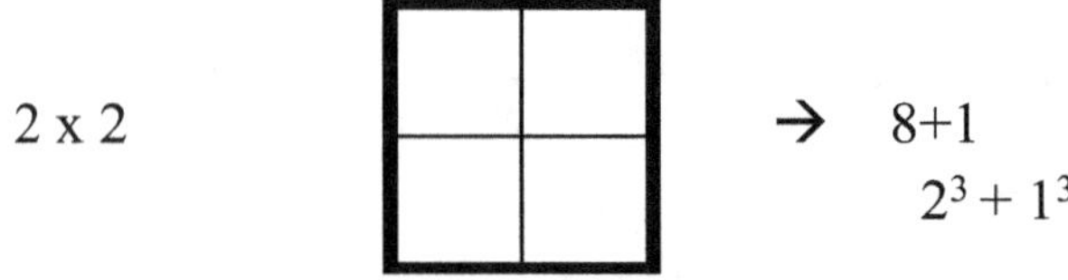

Solution:

1 x 1 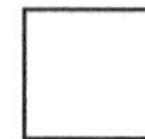 → 1

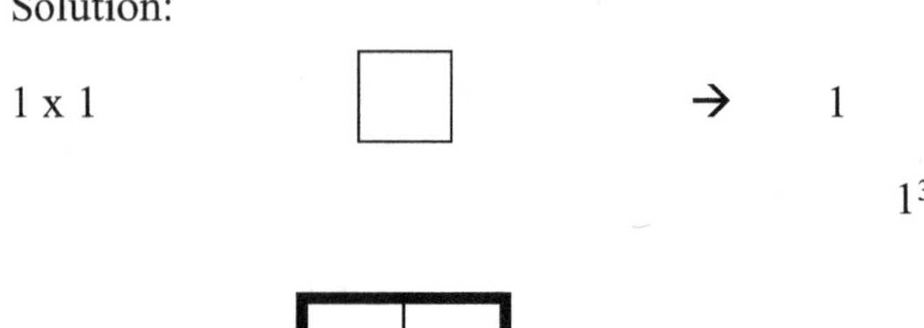

1^3

2 x 2 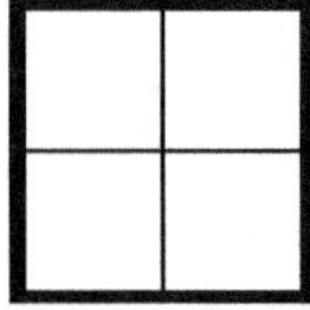 → 8+1

$2^3 + 1^3$

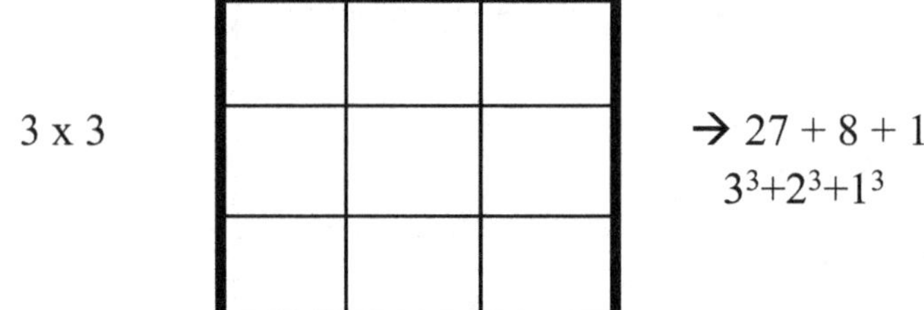

3 x 3 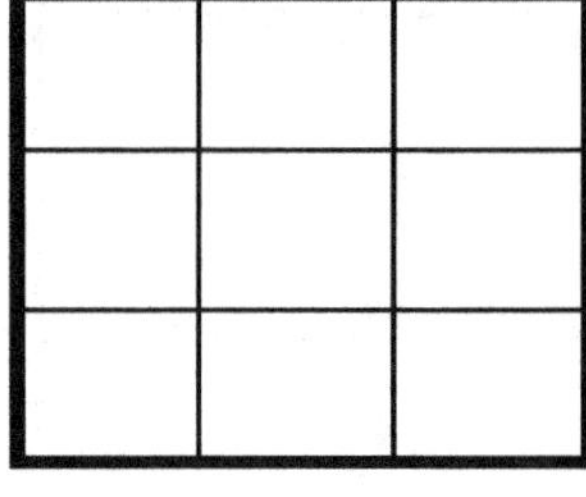 → 27 + 8 + 1

$3^3+2^3+1^3$

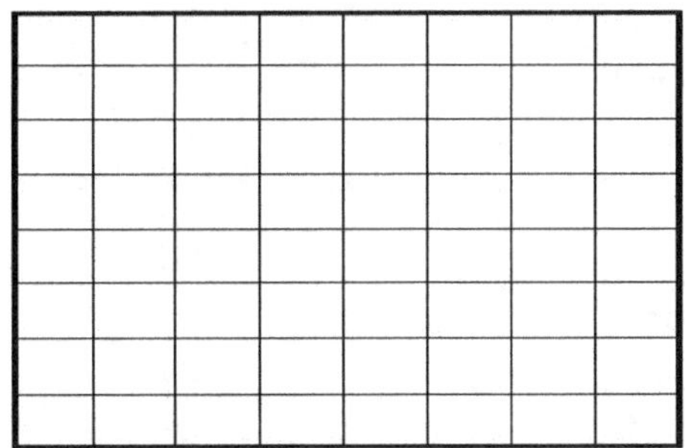

8 x 8 → $1^3 + 2^3 + 3^3 + \ldots\ldots\ldots 8^3$

Here the sequence is sum of Cubes

$$Sum\ of\ cubes\ of\ first\ n\ natural\ numbers = \frac{n^2(n+1)^2}{4}$$

$$1^3 + 2^3 + 3^3 + \ldots\ldots\ldots 8^3 = \frac{8^2(9)^2}{4}$$

$$= 1296$$

Example 4: Find the total number of numbers from 257 to 863

Solution: Take a small set of data to observe the sequence

Numbers between 1-3 → 2 → 3-1 = 2-1 = 1

Numbers between 3-6 → 4, 5 → 6-3 = 3-1 = 2

Numbers between 257-863 → 863-257 → 606-1 = 605

So, 605 numbers are there between 257 and 863.

Example 5: Find the units digit of 9^{891}?

Here we can't find the value of 9^{891} directly so let's take a small set of data. Unit's digit of

9^1 -------- 9

9^2 --------- 1

9^3 -------- 9

9^4 -------- 1

9^5 -------- 9

Here sequence is going on like 9, 1, 9, 1 and so on. If power is odd the answer is '9' and if power is even the answer is '1'.

Example 6: Find the remainder when $7^{629} \div 10$?

$7^1 \div 10 = 7$

$7^2 \div 10 = 9$

$7^3 \div 10 = 3$

$7^4 \div 10 = 1$

$7^5 \div 10 = 7$

$7^6 \div 10 = 9$

$7^3 \div 10 = 3$

Here sequence is going like 7, 9, 3, 1, 7, 9, 3, 1……

So after every four numbers the sequence is going on so divide the power by 4

```
4)629(157
  4
  22
  20
   29
   28
    1
```

So '1' is remainder so 1st number in the sequence is answer.

So the Unit's digit of $(7^{629} \div 10) = 7$

Unit Digit:-

0 → 0

1 → 1

2 → 2, 4, 8, 6

3 → 3, 9, 7, 1

4 → 4, 6

5 → 5

6 → 6

7 → 7, 9, 3, 1

8 → 8, 4, 2, 6

9 → 9

Sequence Categories possible:-

1 Repetition	→	Only one value
2 Repetitions	→	Check power is even or odd
4 Repetitions	→	Divide the power with '4' based on remainder you can fix your answer.

For a four repetition if

Remainder 1	→	First number is the answer
Remainder 2	→	Second number is the answer
Remainder 3	→	Third number is the answer

Remainder 0 → Fourth number is the answer

7. Find the Unit's digit of

$$4^{982} \times 5^{643} \times 7^{491} \times 9^{642} = ?$$

$4^1 = 4$ 5→5 $7^1 = 7$ $9^1 = 9$

$4^2 = 6$ $7^2 = 9$ $9^2 = 1$

$7^3 = 3$

$7^4 = 1$

(……….6) x (……5) x (……..3) x (……..1)

(……….0) x (……3)

(……….0)

So the Unit's digit of $4^{982} \times 5^{643} \times 7^{491} \times 9^{642}$ *is* '0'

Progressions

a) Basic Formulae

$$1 + 2 + 3 + \dots\dots\dots\dots + n = \frac{n\,(n+1)}{2}$$

$$1^2 + 2^2 + 3^2 + \dots\dots\dots\dots + n^2 = \frac{n(n+1)(2n+1)}{6}$$

$$1^3 + 2^3 + 3^3 + \dots\dots\dots\dots + n^3 = \frac{n^2(n+1)^2}{4}$$

b) Arithmetic Progression

Every term after the first term progresses with a common difference'd'.

$$a, a + d, a + 2d \dots\dots\dots\dots, a + (n-1)d$$

Here

a → first term

d → common difference

nth term → a + (n - 1) d

$$Sum\ of\ "n"\ terms \rightarrow \frac{n}{2}[First\ term + last\ term]$$

$$Sum\ of\ "n"\ terms \rightarrow \frac{n}{2}[a + a + (n-1)d] = \frac{n}{2}[2a + (n-1)d]$$

If a, b, and c are in arithmetic progression then

$$b = \frac{a+c}{2}$$

c) Geometric Progression:

Each term after first term is obtained by multiplying or dividing with a fixed number 'r'.

$a, ar^2, ar^3, \ldots\ldots\ldots\ldots\ldots, ar^{(n-1)}$

Here

a → first term

r → common difference

nth term → $ar^{(n-1)}$

Sum of "n" terms → $a(r^n-1)/(r-1)$

Sum of Infinite terms (S_∞) = $a/(1-r)$ where $0<a<1$

If a, b, and c are in Geometric progression then $b^2 = ac$.

d)Harmonic Progression:

The reciprocal of Arithmetic progression is Harmonic Progression.

$$\frac{1}{a}, \frac{1}{a+d}, \frac{1}{a+2d}, \ldots\ldots\ldots\ldots, \frac{1}{a+(n-1)d}$$

N^{th} term of the Sequence (T_n) = $\frac{1}{a+(n-1)d}$

If a,b,c are in Harmonic progression then $b = \frac{2ac}{(a+c)}$

Sets and Venn Diagram

a) List Vs Set

List A = {1, 2, 2, 3, 3, 3, 4}

Set A = {1, 2, 3, 4}

1. In a list repetitions are allowed, but in a set repetitions are not allowed.
2. In a list order matters but in set order doesn't matter.

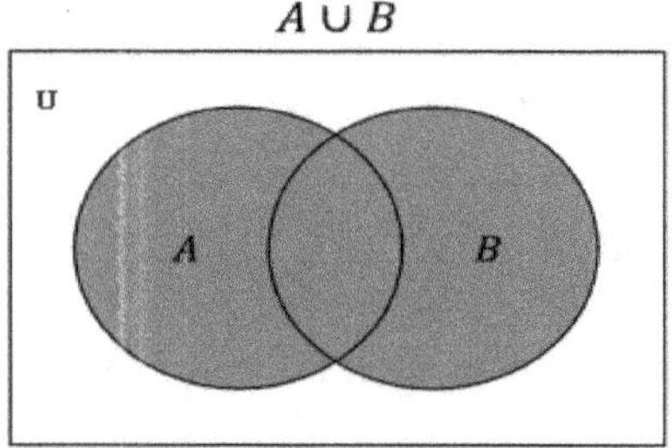

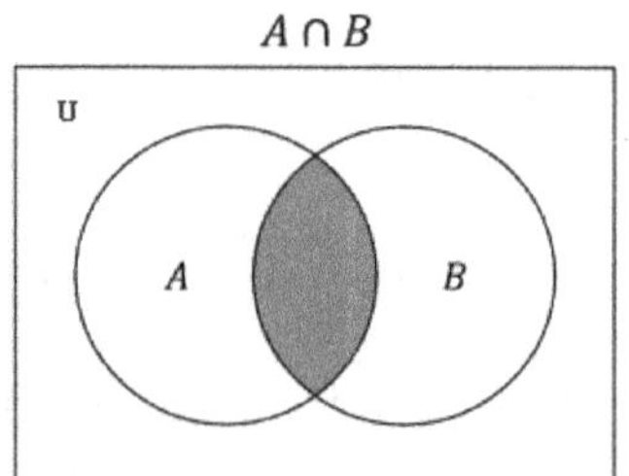

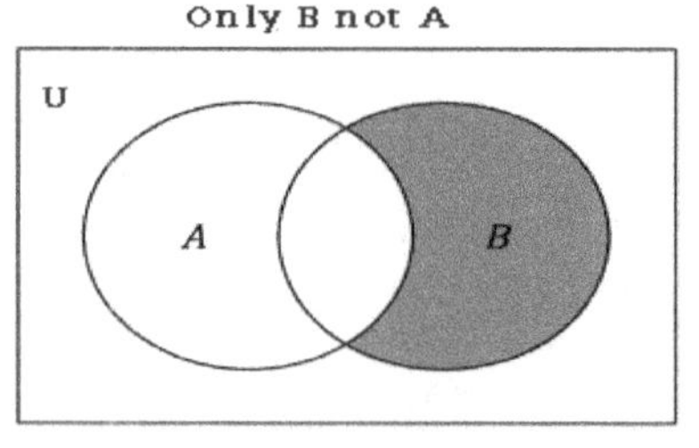

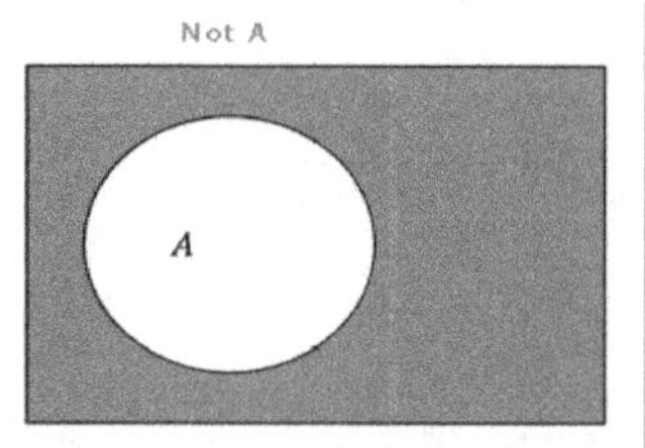

Here U = Universal Set   ϕ = Not A nor B

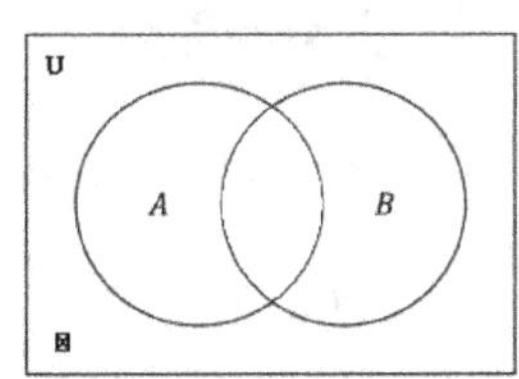

$n(A \cup B) = n(A) + n(B) - n(A \cap B)$

Example: {A} = {1, 2, 3, 4}

No of elements in set A = |A| = 5

Null set =ϕ & |ϕ| =0

b) Disjoint Set:

If two sets contain no common elements they are called as disjoint sets.

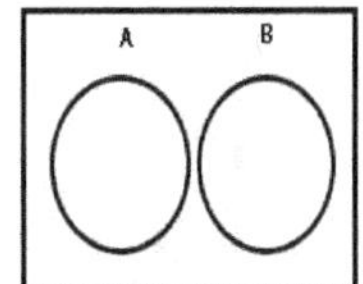

Example:

A = {All even numbers}, B = {All odd numbers}

Here no common elements in A and B so they are disjoint sets.

Subset:

If all elements in 'B' are in 'A' then we say 'B' is subset of 'A'

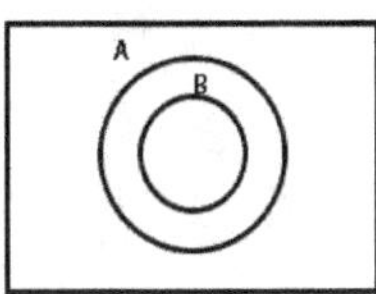

Example:-

A = {All integers}   B = {All positive integers}

c) Types of Question

1. Two sets
2. Three sets
3. Four sets (Grid)

(i)Two Sets

If 2 sets are present in the question we use this.

Venn Diagram Formula

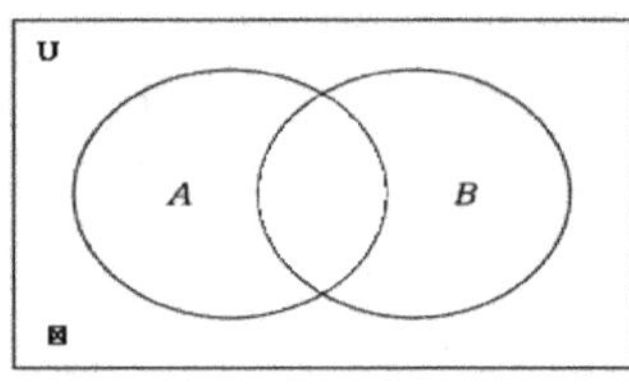

$$n(A \cup B) = n(A) + n(B) - n(A \cap B)$$

Example:

In a class of 40 students 25 play cricket and 15 play football and 5 students neither play football nor cricket then find the number of students who play both games?

Solution:-

Here n(C) = 25 n (F) = 15 None = 5

Here n(C ∪ F) = Total – none
= 40-5
= 35

$$n(C \cup F) = n(C) + n(F) - n(C \cap F)$$

$$35 = 25 + 15 - n(C \cap F)$$

$$n(C \cap F) = 40 - 35$$

$$n(C \cap F) = 5$$

(ii) <u>Three sets</u>

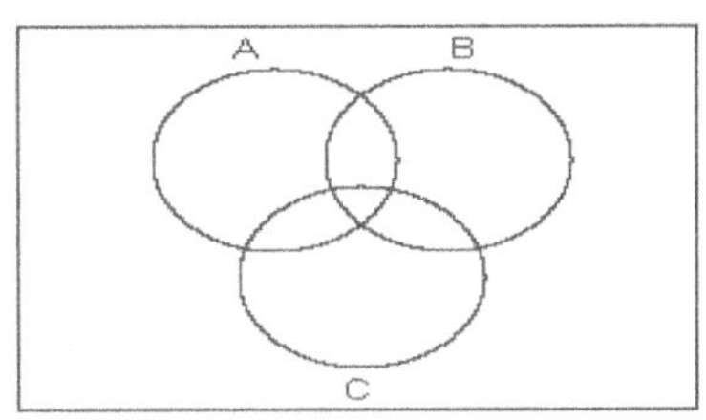

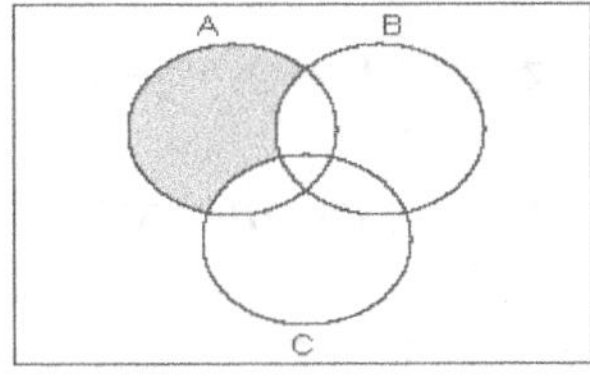

Only 'A'

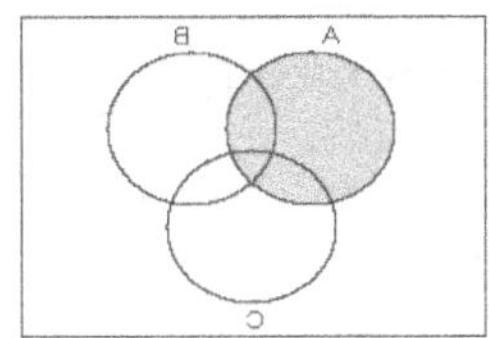

A'

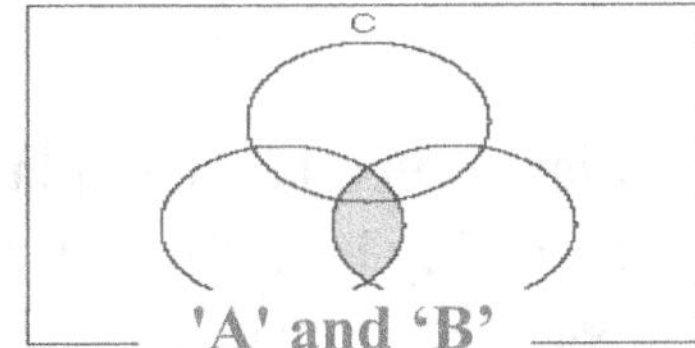

'A' and 'B'

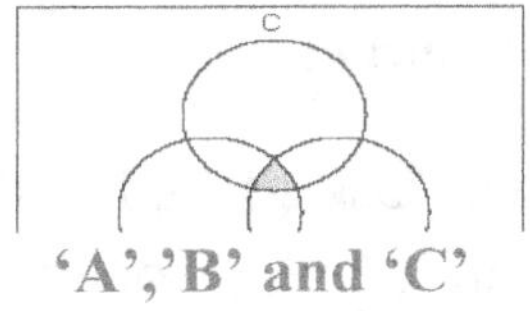

'A','B' and 'C'

(Based on the question we can draw the appropriate Venn diagram and get the answer)

Formula:-

$$n(A \cup B \cup C) = Total\ (\mu) - none$$

$$= n(A) + n(B) + n(C) - n(A \cap B) - n(B \cap C) - n(C \cap A) + n(A \cap B \cap C)$$

$n(A \cup B \cup C) =$

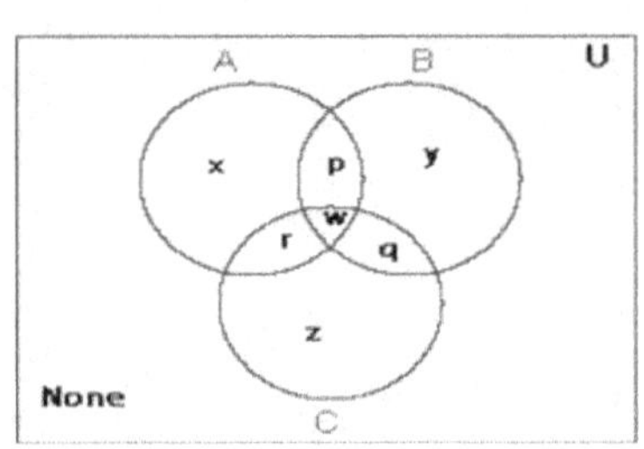

$$\mu - none = n(A \cup B \cup C) = x + y + z + p + q + r + w$$

$x, y, z \rightarrow Elements\ in\ one\ set$

$p, q, r \rightarrow Elements\ in\ two\ sets$

$w \rightarrow Elements\ in\ three\ sets$

Example:-

In a class 20 students play cricket, 25 play football and 30 play tennis, 5 play both cricket and football, 10 play both football and tennis, 8 play both tennis and cricket, 2 play all three games and 12 play none of the three games. Then find the total number of students in the class?

Solution:-

n(c) = 20, n(F) = 25, n(T) = 30, n (C∩F) = 5,

n(F∩T) = 10, n(T∩C) = 8, n(C∩F∩T) = 2, none = 12

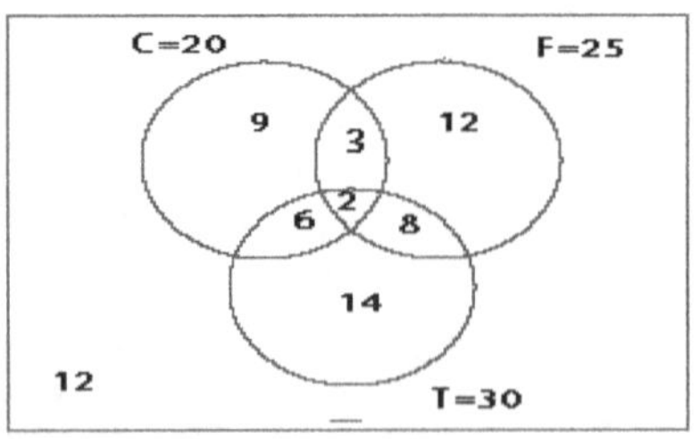

Total = (only in 1 set) + (only in 2 sets) + (only in 3 sets) + none

Total = 9+12+14+3+8+6+2+12 = 66

(iii)<u>Grids:</u>

If there are four different items present in the question we use group grid to solve those problems.

Example:-

In a class there are 500 students, boys are 100 more than total number of girls and 30% of the total girls are vegetarian and ratio of non-vegetarian girls to vegetarian boys is 7:6. Then find the total number of non-vegetarians in the class?

Given: Total = 500

Boys = Girls + 100

Total = B + G

500 = G + 100 + G

500 – 100 = 2G

400 = 2G

200 = G

Girls = 200 Boys = 300

Vegetarian Girls = 30% of 200

$$= \frac{30}{100} \times 200$$

= 60

Non- vegetarian Girls = 200 – 60 =140

	Veg	Non-Veg	Total
Girls	60	140	200
Boys			300
Total			500

N.V (G): V (B) = 7 parts: 6 parts

7 parts = 140 1 part = 20

6 parts = 6 x 20 = 120

	Veg	Non-Veg	Total
Girls	60	140	200
Boys	120	180	300
Total	180	320	500

So the total number of non-vegetarians are 320 students.

(Or)

	Veg	Non-Veg	Total
Girls	30% of G	$7x$	G
Boys	$6x$		G + 100
Total			500

30 % of 200 2G + 100 = 500

$^{30}/_{100} \times 200 = 60$

$$2G = 500 - 100$$

$$2G = 400$$

$$G = 200$$

	Veg	Non-Veg	Total
Girls	30% of G	$7x = 140$ $x = 20$	200
Boys	$6x$		300
Total			500

	Veg	Non-Veg	Total
Girls	60	140	200
Boys	120	180	300
Total	180	320	500

So the total numbers of non-vegetarians are 320 students.

STATISTICS

Statistics

a) Mean:-

Mean and average are one and the same

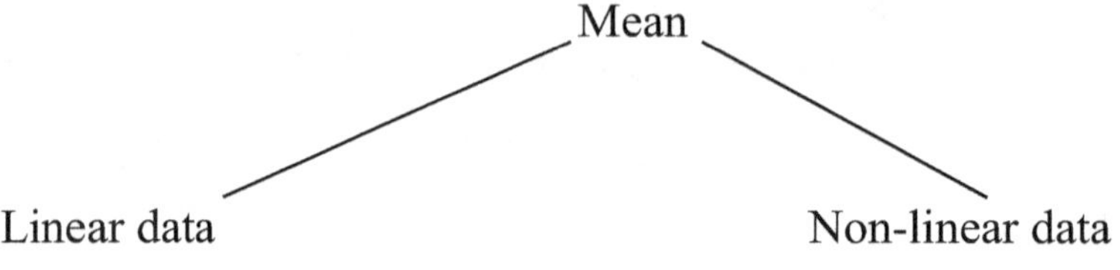

$$Mean = \frac{first\ no + last\ no}{2} \quad Mean = \frac{Sum\ of\ observations}{no\ of\ observations}$$

Mean = middle number (if odd number of values)

Mean = Average of middle numbers (if even no of values)

Example:-

Mean of 5, 7, 9, 11, 13, 15, and 17

$$Mean = \frac{first\ no + last\ no}{2}$$

$$Mean = \frac{5 + 17}{2} = \frac{22}{2} = 11$$

b) Median:-

Median mean after arranging the data in either ascending or descending order

If set contains odd number of numbers

➔ Middle number is median

If set contains even number of numbers

➔ Average of middle number is the median

Example:

8, 3, 5, 13, 15, 9, 11

First arrange

3, 5, 8, 9, 11, 13, 15

9 is Median

Example:

8, 3, 5, 15, 13, 19, 9, 11

Arrange

3, 5, 8, 9, 11, 13, 15, 19

$$Median = \frac{9 + 11}{2} = \frac{20}{2} = 10$$

c) Mode:

Maximum times repeated value in a sequence is called as mode.

Example:

3, 5, 5, 6, 6, 7, 9, 13

5, 6 are modes of data

d) Range:

Difference between Maximum value and minimum value is called as Range.

Example: 2,4,6,7,8,18
Range = 18-2 =16.

e) Standard Deviation:-

The average deviation from mean is called standard deviation.
Steps to find the Standard Deviation

Example:- 1, 5, 3, 7, 9

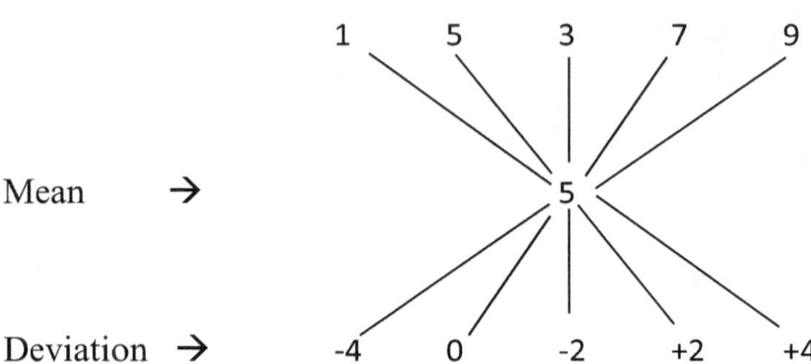

(Average of deviation become zero to avoid it square the deviations)

Square the Deviations → 16, 0, 4, 4, 16

Average → $\frac{16+0+4+4+16}{5} = \frac{40}{5} = 8$

Square root → $\sqrt{8} = 2\sqrt{2}$ (In order to nullity the square we are taking square root)

(Or)

$$Standard\ Deviation = \sqrt{\frac{(\mu - x_1)^2 + (\mu - x_2)^2 + \ldots + (\mu - x_n)^2}{n}}$$

Here $\mu \rightarrow$ *mean* $x_1, x_2 \ldots . x_n \rightarrow$ *values of data and* $n \rightarrow$ *number of items*

f) Normal Distribution:-

This is a statistical analysis not a mathematical value.

Conclusion of survey conducted for students who have taken a test

1. Maximum number of students got their score near to their mean values.
2. Very few students scored maximum mark and very few scored minimum mark.
3. The data when observed appeared like a Bell curve.

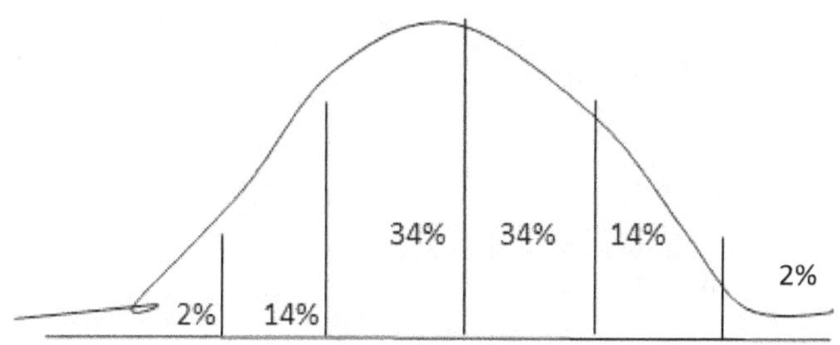

$\mu - 2\sigma \quad \mu - \sigma \quad \mu \quad \mu + \sigma \quad \mu + 2\sigma$

4. We are taking the result as standard values and applicable for all real time observations happening in the universe.

Example:

Let us apply the score on GRE exam taken by 5000 students. Find the standard deviation

Solution:

Minimum score → 260 Maximum score → 340

$$Mean\ score = \frac{260 + 340}{2} = 300$$

Range = Maximum score – Minimum score

= 340 – 260

= 80

For Normal distribution → Range = 6 x Standard Deviation (σ)

$80 = 6 \times S.D\ (\sigma)$

$\frac{80}{6} = S.D\ (\sigma)$

$13\frac{1}{3} = S.D\ (\sigma)$

Now we have

Mean = 300

$S.D\ (\sigma) = 13\frac{1}{3}$

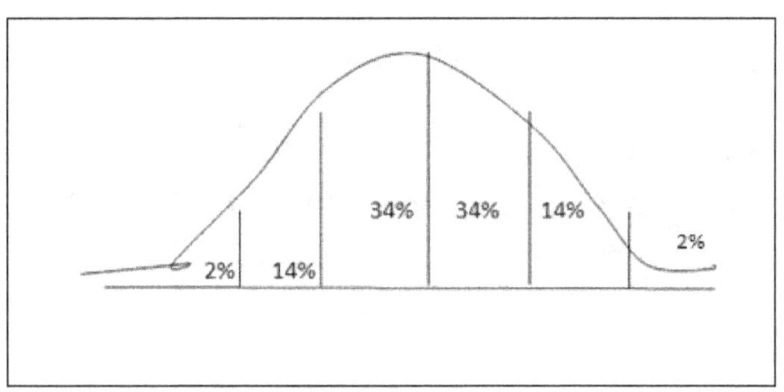

253 1/3 266 2/3 300 313 1/3 326 2/3

It shows

$2\%\ scored\ less\ than\ 253\frac{1}{3}$

$14\% \text{ } scored \text{ } between \text{ } 253\frac{1}{3} - 266\frac{2}{3}$

$34\% \text{ } scored \text{ } between \text{ } 266\frac{2}{3} - 300$

$34\% \text{ } scored \text{ } between \text{ } 300 - 313\frac{1}{3}$

$14\% \text{ } scored \text{ } between \text{ } 313\frac{1}{3} - 326\frac{2}{3}$

$2\% \text{ } scored \text{ } greater \text{ } than \text{ } 326\frac{2}{3}$

Out of 5000 students who scored greater than $313\frac{1}{3} = 14\% + 2\% = 16\%$

➔ $16\% \text{ } of \text{ } 5000 = \frac{16}{100} \times 5000 = 800$

g) Percentile

What is the difference between percentage and percentile?

- ➔ Percentages are calculated on the total marks
- ➔ Percentiles are calculated on the rank obtained in a group (based on median score)
- ➔ Highest scorer is awarded 100% (Percentiles) and next rank comes in that order.

h) Quartiles

While finding the quartiles first arrange the data in ascending order and find the median and proceed continuously.

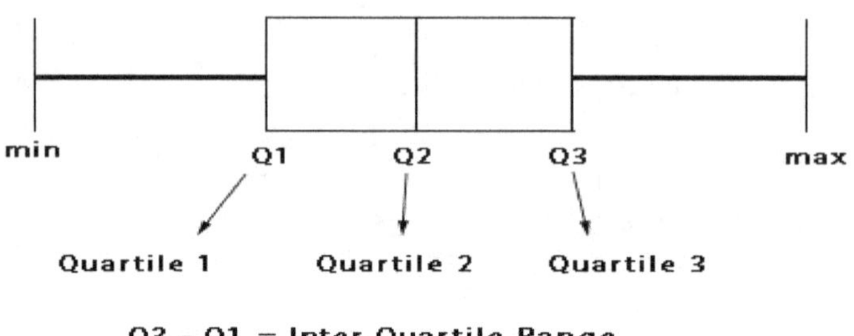

Example:- Find the Q1, Q2, Q3 and interquartile Range for the given data

3, 8, 6, 3, 2, 1, 5, 9, 14, 17, 12, 9, 13, 15 20

Solution:-Arrange data in ascending order

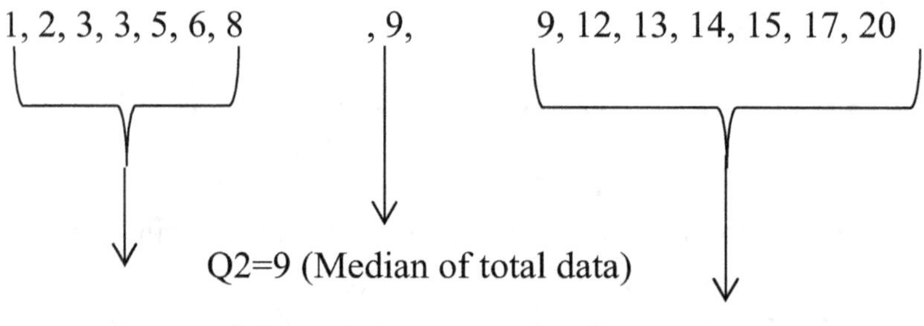

Q1=3 (Median of first data) Q3=14(Median of last data)

1, 2, 3, 3, 5, 6, 8, 9, 9, 12, 13, 14, 15, 17, 20

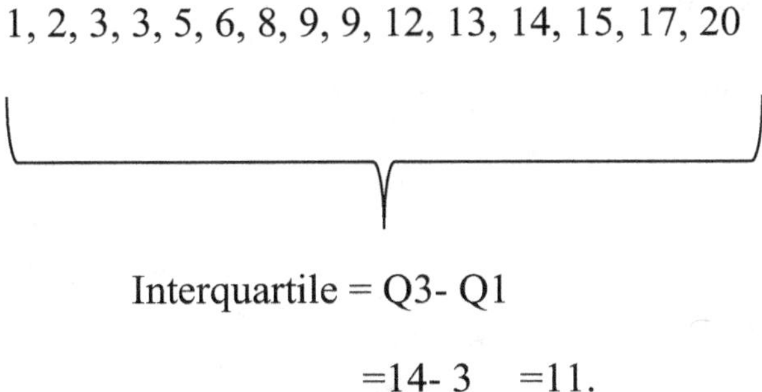

Interquartile = Q3- Q1

=14- 3 =11.

Data Interpretation

This is a type of question in arithmetic where we need to solve the questions by using the details given in the Charts. Different types of figures you find in the exam are:

Tabular form

Bar Graphs

Pie charts

Line Graphs

Multiple Graphs

(i) Basic Approach to solve:

1. Analyze the graph (Try to identify all the things Graphs are taking about).

2. Identify the scale given on the Graph.

3. In case of multiple Graphs try to identify the relation between both the figures.

4. Read the question and note down all the information you require from the graph.

5. Go to graph and get the required data.

6. Use the appropriate formulas and get the answers.

7. Don't waste time on time taking questions. Try to solve the easy question first.

(ii) Types of question:

Different types of question you can find in data interpretation are

Basic arithmetic (+, -, x, /)

Percentages

Ratios

Averages

Comparison Questions

Examples:

Question No 1

In a class there are 5 students and each student has taken the test for 5 subjects and the score of the students is shown below:

	A	B	C	D	E
S1	90	60	90	30	65
S2	75	50	95	60	50
S3	30	85	100	35	45

S4	45	90	70	80	70
S5	70	40	40	75	80

(Note: If a student scored less than or equal to 35 marks in any of the subject he is considered as fail. And each exam was considered for 100 marks)

1. Find the percentage of scored obtain by 'D'?

Solution:

$$Percentage\ of\ D = \frac{Mark\ obtain\ by\ "D"}{Total\ marks} \times 100$$

$$Percentage\ of\ D = \frac{30 + 60 + 35 + 80 + 75}{500} \times 100$$

$$Percentage\ of\ D = \frac{280}{500} \times 100$$

$$Percentage\ of\ D = \frac{280}{5}$$

$$Percentage\ of\ D = 56\%$$

2. Find the average marks obtained by the student in subject 'S_2'?

Solution:

$$Average\ mark\ in\ S_2 = \frac{Total\ mark\ in\ S_2}{No\ of\ students}$$

$$Average\ mark\ in\ S_2 = \frac{75 + 50 + 95 + 60 + 50}{5}$$

$$Average\ mark\ in\ S_2 = \frac{330}{5}$$

$$Average\ mark\ in\ S_2 = 66\ Marks$$

3. Find the pass percentage of the class.

Solution: Given if a student scored less than or equal to 35 marks in any subject is called as fail.

Here student 'A' and 'D' are failed students and 'B', 'C' and 'E' passed in all subjects.

$$Pass\ Percentage = \frac{No\ of\ student\ passed}{total\ no\ of\ student} \times 100$$

$$Pass\ Percentage = \frac{3}{5} \times 100$$

$$Pass\ Percentage = \frac{300}{5}$$

$$Pass\ Percentage = 60\%$$

4. Find the student who scored 2nd highest marks in the class?

Solution:

A = 90+73+30+45+70= 310

B = 60+50+85+90+40= 325

C = 90+95+100+70+40= 395

D = 30+60+35+80+75= 280

E = 65+50+45+70+80= 310

So 'B' scored highest score in the class.

5. Find the ratio of score of student A to rest of the students in the class?

Solution:

→ (Score of student A): (Score of B, C, D, E)

→ 310: (325 + 395 + 280 + 310)

→ 310: 1310

→ 31: 131

Question No 2

Score obtained by the student in different subjects and the student scored 560 marks in Science subject:

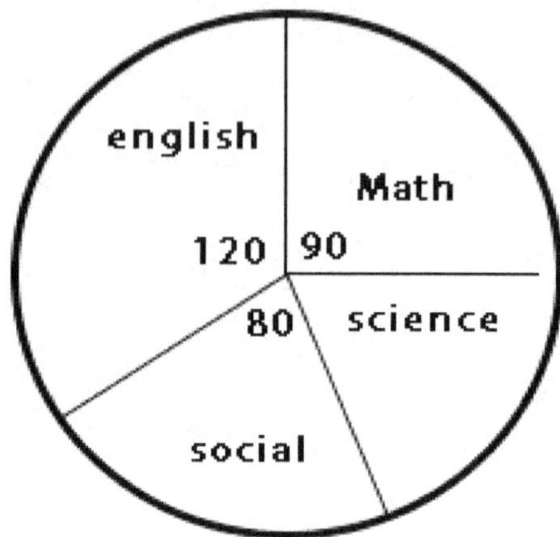

Distibution of Score in Different Subjects

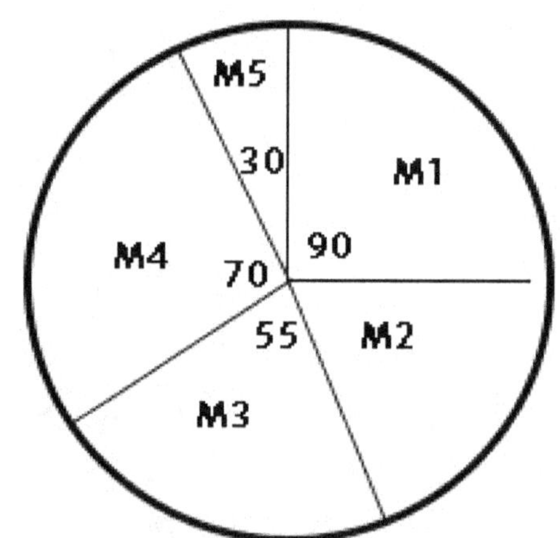

Distribution of score in math ssubject

Basic Analysis of the question:

1. Relation between both the charts is math portion of 1st Pie-chart represents the complete 2nd Pie-chart.

Chart 1 :

2. Here 560 marks are the total score in science subject.

Here Degree measure of science = 360^0 - (100 + 90 + 80)

= 360^0 -290^0

= 70^0

So 70^0 = 560 marks

$$1^0 = \frac{560}{70} = 8 \text{ Marks.}$$

Chart 2:

3. 90^0 both of the first chart represents 360^0 of second chart so

1^0 = ¼ (8 marks) = 2 marks

So in second chart 1^0 = 2 marks.

1. Find the score of the student in subject M_4?

Solution: In second chart

1^0 = 2 marks

So M4 score = 70^0 x 2 = 140 marks

2. Find the ratio of scores of social to M_2?

Solution:

(Score of social): (Score of M_2)

80^0 in first pie-chart: 115^0 in second pie-chart

80^0 x 8: 115^0 x 2

640: 230

64: 23

3. What percentage of total score is the score of M_5?

Solution:

$$\% \, score \, of \, M_5 = \frac{score \, in \, "M_5"}{Total \, score} \times 100$$

$$\% \, score \, of \, M_5 = \frac{30 \times 2}{360 \times 8} \times 100$$

$$\% \, score \, of \, M_5 = 2 \, \%$$

4. What percentage is the score in social greater than the score in M_4?

Solution:

Social $= 80^0$ x 8 $=$ 640

M_4 $= 70^0$ x 2 $=$ 140

$$\% \, greater = \frac{change}{orginal} \times 100$$

$$\% \, greater = \frac{640 - 140}{140} \times 100$$

$$\% \, greater = \frac{500}{140} \times 100$$

$$\% \, greater = \frac{2500}{7}$$

$$\% \ greater = 357\,{}^{1}/_{7}\% \ greater$$

5. Find the Average score of English, M_1, M_2 and M_3?

Solution:

English	$= 120^0 \times 8 = 960$
M_1, M_2 and M_3	$= 260^0 \times 2 = 520$
Total	$=$ 1480

$$Average = \frac{total\ score}{number} = \frac{1480}{4} = 370\ marks$$

Question No 3

Production of food grain in different years

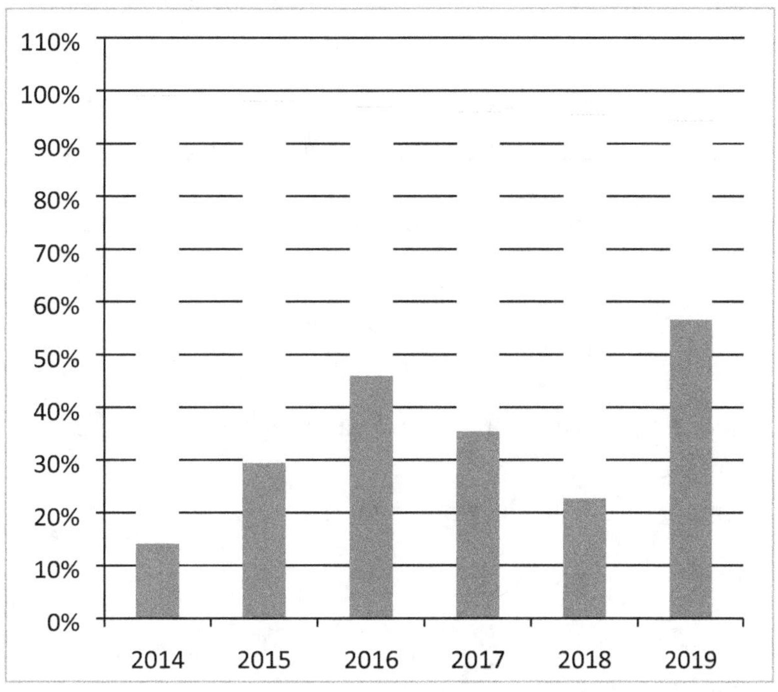

Scale on y-axis 1 Unit =500 tons

1. Find the percentage increase in the production of food grains from 2014 to 2015?

Solution: $$\% \, change = \frac{change}{orginal} \times 100$$

$$\% \, change = \frac{30 - 15}{15} \times 100$$

$$\% \, change = \frac{15}{15} \times 100$$

$$\% \, change = 1 \times 100$$

$$\% \, change = 100\%$$

2. Find the ratio of production of food grains from odd years to even
years?

Solution: (2015, 2017, 2019): (2014, 2016, 2018)

(30 + 35 + 60): (15 + 45 + 25)

125: 85

25: 17

3. Among the given years where can you find the highest percentage
increase in the production of food grains?

Solution:

By observing the chart you can see a highest percentage increase from 2018 to 2019

2018 → 25 2019 → 60

$$\% \, increase = \frac{change}{orginal} \times 100$$

$$\% \, change = \frac{60 - 25}{25} \times 100$$

$$\% \, change = \frac{35}{25} \times 100$$

$$\% \, change = 140\%$$

4. Find the average production of food grains during the years 2015,
2017 and 2018?

Solution:

2015 → 30

2017 → 35

2018 → 25

$$Average = \frac{30 + 35 + 25}{3}$$

$$Average = \frac{90}{3}$$

$$Average = 30$$

On y-axis 1 unit is 500 tons.

So average production = 30 x 500 = 1500 tons

5. Find the average percentage increase in the production from 2014 to 2019?

Solution:

2014 → 15 2019 → 60

$$\% \, increase = \frac{change}{orginal} \times 100$$

$$\% \, change = \frac{60 - 15}{15} \times 100$$

$$\% \, change = \frac{45}{15} \times 100$$

$$\% \, change = 300\%$$

Average increased means from 2014-2019

There are 5 changes

2014 → 15, 2015 → 16, 2016 → 17, 2017 → 18, 2018 →19

$$\% \, increase = \frac{\% \, increase}{No \, of \, Changes}$$

$$\% \, increase = \frac{300\%}{5}$$

$$\% \, increase = 60\%$$

www.ingramcontent.com/pod-product-compliance
Lightning Source LLC
Chambersburg PA
CBHW071414150726
48000CB00001B/321

* 9 7 9 8 6 4 6 6 0 1 1 6 3 *